THE DISSIDENT PROPHET

By

BIJAN PEDRAM

Foreword

In The Dissident Prophet, Bijan Pedram invites us into a deeply personal and expansive journey—a life shaped by revolution, exile, love, and relentless hope. From the bustling bazaars of Ahwaz during wartime to the quiet reflections of a poet in distant lands, Pedram's poetry pulses with the lifeblood of memory and the enduring spirit of resilience.

Dedication

I dedicate this poetry collection to my beloved homeland, Iran, and to the shared experiences that connect us all as human beings.

I also dedicate this work to my wonderful wife, Shida,

And my beautiful family: Shayun, Shiva, Shabnam, DJ, Nico, and Cyrus with all my love, I cherish each of you.

Acknowledgment

I would like to express my heartfelt gratitude to my beloved wife, Shida. You are not only the love of my life but also the very muse that inspires my creativity and fuels my passion for poetry. To my wonderful children, Shabnam, Shiva, and Shayun, you are the three bright stars of my life. Your presence and unwavering encouragement have been instrumental in my artistic journey, and your belief in me has kept the creative spark alive.

I am deeply thankful to my mother, whose sweet songs have always filled my heart, and to my father, who introduced me to the love of writing poetry. Your support in providing me with the time and space to cultivate my craft has been invaluable.

I would also like to extend my heartfelt appreciation to my brother Massoud, who has been a guiding light through the ordeals of life in exile with his wisdom and unwavering love. Massoud, without your presence and support, I would never have dared to seek a harbor of tranquility in my life.

To my dear friend Nader Niakan, you are not only my best friend but also the one who saved my life more than once. We are like one soul in two bodies, having experienced both the joys and ordeals of life together. Your unwavering support and camaraderie have enriched my journey in ways that words cannot fully express.

Last but not least, I want to extend my gratitude to my other friends, Hamid Koochak Entezar and Masi Sari. Your willingness to engage with my work and provide thoughtful feedback has been invaluable, and I truly appreciate the time you invested in discussing my poems with me.

Lastly, I extend my gratitude to KDP Publishing, who skillfully edited my poems and provided invaluable guidance throughout this journey. Your expertise has helped shape my writing in ways I could not have achieved alone.

Thank you all for being a part of this journey.

About the Author

I am a poet shaped by a life filled with profound highs and challenging lows. My journey began in Iran, where I enthusiastically participated in the 1979 Iranian Revolution, driven by hope for change. However, this fervor quickly turned into disillusionment as I witnessed the rise of an oppressive regime. My activism led to the cessation of my university education and the loss of my social rights as a citizen, making me a target of persecution.

During the tumultuous Iran-Iraq War, I experienced chaos firsthand in my hometown of Ahwaz. One vivid memory that stands out is the day I watched my community struggle to find normalcy amidst the turmoil of bombings that heavily affected the bazaar. Years later, in 1986, in search of a brighter future, I left Iran to pursue my studies abroad. My path took me to Karachi, where I worked with the UNHCR for two years, helping those in need while navigating my own challenges. It was during this time that I married the love of my life, Shida, my twin flame and a source of strength and inspiration.

Eventually, I migrated to Canada, where I pursued my education in chemistry. My time in Toronto was filled with the joy of welcoming three beautiful children into our family. As I embraced fatherhood, I learned the true meaning of resilience and hope. Our journey continued as we moved to California, where I contributed to major pharmaceutical companies, focusing on drug discovery—a field that allows me to merge my scientific passion with the desire to make a difference.

Throughout the last 45 years, I have penned these poems, reflecting the myriad experiences that have shaped my understanding of life, love, resilience, and the bitterness of exile. Each piece serves as a testament to the complexities of my journey and the hope that continues to guide me toward my ambition for peace and freedom for all humankind—living in harmony, free from oppression and social pain.

As I share my poetry, I hope to inspire others to embrace their own journeys with courage and compassion, reminding them that they are loved and not alone.

About the Book

I said: what about my eyes?

He said: Keep them on the road.

I said: What about my passion?

He said: Keep it burning.

I said: What about my heart?

He said: Tell me what you hold inside it?

I said: Pain and sorrow.

He said: Stay with it. The wound is the place where the Light enters you.

- Maulana Rumi-

This anthology, a collection of transformative poetry, intertwines themes of life, love, loss, and regeneration. It is divided into twenty thematic sections, each encapsulating poignant sentiments that resonate universally. Spanning various periods of Bijan Pedram's career, the book chronicles the evolution of his voice—where youthful exuberance meets the reflections of seasoned introspection.

The titles alone evoke the essence of the human experience: "*A Bitter Verse*," "*A Goblet of Memories*," "*A Lament of Sorrow*," and "*The End*," are just a hint of what awaits within these pages. The reader will encounter a rich exploration of love in all its forms—exuberant, nostalgic, ephemeral, and eternal.

The imagery within the poems runs deep, capturing brief moments of beauty intertwined with an undercurrent of melancholy. Nature becomes both a backdrop and a character, offering solace and pain alike. Readers are gently encouraged to pause and reflect on their own relationships, memories, and the echo of their own voices that may lie dormant within.

In this world of poetic verses, language dances like the shadows under the moonlight—a truly immersive experience. It is

a call to those who appreciate the beauty of words, those who relish the complexity of emotional depth, and those who seek to understand the resonance of being alive.

Prepare to lose yourself in the transformative power of Pedram's poetry as it unfolds the myriad layers of your heart, leading you to new understandings of love, loss, and the intricate dance of existence. Each poem carries the weight of a history rich with feeling, waiting for your gaze to bring it back to life once more.

Preface

"In the depth of winter, I finally learned that within me there lay an invincible summer."

- Albert Camus essay "Return to Tipasa"

In the vast expanse of human experience, I find an intricate tapestry woven with threads of love, loss, longing, and the quest for meaning. As you turn the pages of this anthology, I hope you will join me on a journey through the poignant landscapes of emotion and memory that resonate with the soul's deepest ambivalence.

Drawing from the ancient pulse of Persian literature while embracing contemporary existence, I have crafted this collection of verses with the hope that it invites you to linger in the delicate balance between despair and hope. Each poem is intended to serve as a mirror, reflecting the complexity of our human condition and revealing the multifaceted interplay between light and shadow, joy and sorrow.

As you explore these lyrical pages, may the words wrap around you like a tender embrace, guiding you through the misty corridors of memory and desire. A sense of intimacy pervades every line, encouraging an introspective communion with the heart's deepest yearnings. Here, you will encounter the winding paths of affection, the vibrant colors of nature, and the silent echoes of loss that resonate within us all.

This journey is not merely about passive reading; it is an invitation to feel, to contemplate, and to connect with your own hidden emotions. I invite you to prepare for the emotional ebb and flow of these verses, as they beckon you to embrace the complexities of love and the bittersweet nature of existence. With heartfelt anticipation, I welcome you to embark upon this voyage through the indelible impressions left by the human heart.

Bijan Pedram

March 20, 2025

Table of Contents

A Bitter Verse

Birds raise their songs to greet the crisp dawn air,
Unaware that you're not there to share their prayer.

Blossoms unfurl gracefully upon the boughs,
Ignorant of your absence, and how it sows.

And children, whimsical, grasp the playful breeze,
Oblivious to the laughter lost, how it flees.

Your absence sows a sorrow deep within my core,
Melting into a thirst more fierce than the sun's own roar—

Without the song's sweet plea, the dance of growth,
Or the merry prance of life's gentle oath.

A fleeting smile to grace my lips is rare,
Knowing you are not here, you are not there,

You are simply… nowhere. ...and nowhere,
for all eternity, you'll be nowhere.

Dedicated to Shahrokh Zargar and his enduring epic.

A Dwelling Enveloped in Mist

I can scarcely fathom the expanse of this mist,

How it softly envelops the doors and walls of this dwelling.

I can scarcely fathom, dear deity,

to whom shall I confide this?

A trepidation lingers within my heart of life's duplicitous ways,

for what shrouds so densely may not truly be the mist.

Yet the wisps and sighs of an impassioned, tormented lover,

Consumed by the flames of an abiding love. Linger here

A lover scorched upon the doorknob,

whose gaze no longer heeds

the sound of approaching footsteps.

Though in my heart, but his heart is not with me.

With him, a fire ignites within my soul,

and between me and each window,

a dense smoke ascends.

At times I contemplate,

perhaps the bond between solitude and mist

is why it's so hard for me

to embark on a sojourn and relinquish my existence.

At times I muse,

if only on a frigid morn,

I could shoulder my knapsack, and tread a path

to abandon the smoke and burdensome mists that enshroud me,

towards distant horizons

and harmonious melodies that beckon me

From the anthology "Lost in the Wind"
March 13, 2004

A Goblet of Memories

The air brims with a dream, dissolved in the wind,
a childlike longing saturates the lost orchard lanes.
Narcissus and white jasmines abound on mountain slopes,
scenting the breeze with their inviting blooms.

There is a gentle, maternal essence woven through the air,
leading us, with a mother's smile, to a welcoming dawn—
a breakfast of bread, cheese, and sweet tea shared.

A father's anxious gaze lingers on the doorstep,
watching over his young child with unease,
brushing every lock tangled by the teasing breeze.
He whispers to himself:
"Oh, my child,
the wind may whisk you away,
as a delicate fairy flutters from a blossoming spray."

The air whispers of earth, washed clean by rain,
covering a mother's gaze with the shroud of death,
softening a father's calloused hands with its tender touch.

****

The earth is drunk on the scent of rain-kissed soil,
and the soil on the delightful aroma of your dancing steps,
on a melancholy night, in the drizzle's embrace.

Night is overcome with the fragrance of jasmine,
and the jasmine with the perfume of your breath,
as you sleep upon a bed of nocturnal dreams.
Waves of light, set in motion by your charming presence,
transform the chilly dawn into a symphony of silk melodies,
unraveling silently, inviting the meadow's bloom,
as butterfly wings tenderly welcome the flowered plains.

****

Night is the seed of beginnings,
the bed of solitude,
a majestic, soul-piercing modesty,
reposed on its crag of isolation,
unfolding to the compelling songs of myriad birds,
in the soft caress of your breath,
with sweet memories lingering.

Night holds the cold silence of jasmine,
and the butterflies, deep in slumber.
It is the wild rush of the wind,
the harsh screech of owls
in a graveyard fallen from remembrance
unless you, and only you, tread the path.

The earth, laying bare its flesh,
yearns for your footsteps,

to the rhythm of the rain's caress.

A child's tousled hair

has long been plundered by a damp zephyr.

The earth lies in wait, just as he,

for you to approach the door

with a goblet of memories in hand

and a garment of freshly bloomed jasmines and narcissus,

veiling the grace of your nude beauty.

It waits for you

to step through the door

and dance with the wind,

to weave the threads of our past

into the fabric of the night,

where memories and dreams entwine,

and every heartbeat echoes

the warmth of what was,

as we embrace the dawn together,

forever in the light.

Lament of Agony

Mourning echoes, anguished cries kick dust,
Blood streams weave down faces, a sorrowful flood,
Countless mothers wail for children silenced in slaughter.

While the innocent weep,
For the sweet milk of comfort now dried in deserted veins,
As women await death, bound to the noose's embrace,
Longing for the children they won't hold again.

The nation's people, shackled, lament and howl,
Homeland hung high, and their grief—
A river mighty, eroding stone,
Carves the canyons of men's eyes, brands their brows
With unspeakable terrors,
And on the grace of young maidens,
A wide channel of blood etched deep.

***

Agony they raise,
Their cries rend the heavens,
Plucking hairs from their weeping scalps
At abundant tombs, unnumbered.

Speak not to me,
Desire not of me,
To drown in ethereal love
When a brother, for the 'crime' of love, is led to captivity.
And weary shoulders abandon their burden on towering pillars,
Leaning back,
Drawing smoke,
Retreating into oneself,
While vicious hands of wind play upon the pole,
Claiming a sister's lifeless body as a toy.

***

Ah,
My sister unshrouded!
The cries I hear.

Alas

Oh my, oh my, She slips away,

Fading before my very eyes, Like a weary moon's body,

That wanes with each passing night.

In wintry slumber, lost in darkness, No hearth,

No lantern,

Nor even the blind guide of a glowworm. She slips from my grasp,

Like a young dove, Longing to take flight, But striking a stone, And with her,

Countless desires cradled in a mother's heart.

Oh my, oh my,

Like an unread letter on its way, Bound by the feet of a dove,

This heart of mine slips away with her, And shall not return

To the sanctuary of my chest again.

Oh, if only!

Oh, if only,

I could escape this nightmare, And awaken to a morning,

Where she would remain with me. Oh, time, slow your pace,

Oh, earth, cease your futile turns, So I may not witness a moment,

When this enchanting, captivating beauty, No longer resides by my side,

Laughing and frolicking on this world.

Oh my, oh my, Where is it, where?

That poisonous charm they speak of?

Where is that venomous pleasure they mention? Oh, time, slow your pace, linger.

Or place me upon the shoulder of this caravan, whisk me away with her, So I may not witness a moment when she is gone.

Oh my, oh my…

From the collection "In Exile"

January 25, 2017

A Very Short Story

It's noon,
a warm noon,
with sunlight spilling down,
narrow alleys whisper secrets,
crooked houses lean with tales untold,
and a dry anticipation lingers
on the doorknobs, waiting.

Oh, blue cloud,
tell me a story
in your soft, drizzling rain,
each drop a note, a memory,
a gentle caress of yearning,
drenching the earth in dreams,
awakening the silence
that cradles the heart.

Let the rhythm of your fall
unravel the threads of time,
weaving together moments
lost in the past,
for in your embrace,
I seek the beauty
that only the sky can share.

From the collection "In the Desire for Flight"

September 1986 – Karachi

Altruism

To you, my dear friend, her unwavering love,

A light that shines, profound as the endless sky;

She set you free, a bittersweet farewell,

Yet in her departure, her heart whispered hope:

That you would climb, as a wave crests toward the sun,

To sacrifice deeply, beyond the horizon of your dreams.

From the collection "Voices of Passion"

January 1988, Karachi

Alas, my plight

As my father departed,
my heart crumbled within.
When my mother passed,
she took all my heart's reserves
with her in ascent.

Now I stand,
empty-handed,
with nothing to offer—
no beating heart,
only silence echoing
in the chambers of my soul.

Alas, for me!
Alas, for me!
I am rendered hollow:
hands that grasp at shadows,
a heart that lies barren,
a home, a garden,
all stripped of life,
devoid of love.

Each day drags on,
a whisper of what once was,
and I wander through this desolate space,

searching for remnants,
for a flicker of warmth,
but finding only echoes
of laughter long gone.

From the collection "In Search of My Land"
April 4, 2018

A Minstrel's Ballade

A wandering bard, with features wan,

pallid as the moon in veil,

beneath a cloud-laden dawn,

with an ancient instrument, tales to unveil.

A retired captain of a ship,

a master of chants,

sans craft or oar,

unenvying his scanty grants,

his hat a tale unspoken,

for the sea's heart, he sings offshore.

Seated carefree, untroubled by fate,

unfazed by his essence or absence here,

not mourning yesterdays too late,

nor dreading tomorrows drawing near.

A draught of wine in clay detained,

he croons alongside a broken lyre—

as fractured as his stature waned,

the force of his once commanding fire.

People rush by, diverted,

as gusts shepherd lost vessels

in a frigid bugle, silently concerted;

from shore to shore, their pace unsettles.

Yet the skipper, for the sea's mighty will, performs

in tattered garbs hugged to his skin,

his voice—a warm wave, it transforms,

thawing ice through the city's veins so thin.

"Ponds, O heart,

can be clothed in old vestments,

or dried and set apart.

A verdant forest, O heart,

might shed its green threads bare,

or be consumed by flame's chart.

But you, O heart,

O heart,

O heart."

With an old lyre in hand,

and a voice that, if heeded, would charm

the air's finest band;

but the people flowed, transient goals,

like ants in fervent march,

lacking patience for a still pause—

to linger, embrace, and let charm arch

the beauty within his voice's cause.

The late morn blossomed on the path

in silence left bereft

of the old voyager's musical wrath,

on the way, a captain deft.

With a cold smile upon his lips,

an aged lyre in tight grasp—

his face, colorless from winter's eclipse,

lies in a sleep that no longer has clasp.

He journeys to meet the sea's mighty call,

his hat, though bare,

on the shoulders of the wind, it falls,

to the sight of seas fair and rare.

From the collection "In Exile"

September 28, 2016

Amid Fleeting Joys

Within yearning hearts, our spirits find their space,
Like orbs of grape, sacred, suspended in time's embrace.
Bathed in the caress of a summer dawn aglow,
Emerald drops ripening, heralds of hope they show.

Souls adrift, we join in a hallowed throng,
Vibrant as winter's pomegranate, bold and strong.
A solitary heart, unfurled in vulnerability,
Craving connection's touch, seeking kin's affinity.

Yet in the quietude of shared glances, I stand,
Neither confining affection nor silencing words at hand,
For your beaming allure has graced my view,
Melodies myriad my lips have inherited from you.

My exultation blooms in the clutch of vernal promise,
Where dreams entwine with swallows, awash in solace.
Snowflakes kissed by tender palms, gentle and benign,
Through your soft encounters, it's your essence that aligns.

Strolling together toward life's fruitful bower,
We listen as verdant clusters impart their power:
"Existence transcends this, denies these brimming eyes,
Not housed in sorrow's upheaval or inward cries.

Existence mirrors the wine within our spirit's carafe,

Becomes acrid and skewed, should grief weave its chaff."

An Assault on the Mist

Morning mist, a chilly embrace,

envelops my home so tight,

that joy feels out of place.

Now a sepulchral space, a den of delusion,

our cheer-forged abode transformed by confusion.

Alas, if only,

in the heart, cloaked by layers of fog,

where you have lost your trace,

I had not feared its grim, ashen face.

In that enveloping haze, shouldering your fears,

I'd walk beside you, whispering courage in your ears.

I wish you had told me

on that mist-veiled day,

that a sharp spear sought your kindred heart in blood.

Beware! For hope of seeing you again fades,

yet yearning lingers in my heart,

wishing for a path cleared

to the sunbeam of hope nested inside you.

Within this hallucinatory cave, I seek

symbols of our togetherness, our joy, one more time.

If only there were a way,

side by side with you, without delay,

on that path anew, to take flight

toward horizons winged in ascending light.

A New Song

And ever comes spring,
sans someone's visage to behold,
down-trodden paths it weaves,
where in your heart's enclave,
a bed—eternally unfurled.

Forever, yes, ever,
a vernal whisper calls,
entreating you to sing again—
melodies of deep longing,
tender love songs, necessity's thrall,
a true heart's chorus in the sparrows' hall.

So it goes, this age-old norm, my dear:
spring, with its perennial cue,
beckons you to kiss life anew,
to love, to let your spirit soar.
Though in another fall, silence your lore,
standing quiet beside a lost one's grave—
yet another love, unspoken, unsaved.

From the collection "Lost in the Wind"
March 1997, Toronto

Anticipation

A deep freeze, steadfast, pierces the core, Dimming eyes' luster

To a subdued shimmer on iced veneer, Where the night's jeweled circlet

Fixes its crystalline stare, Right into my reflection.

Allied with the relentless wilds, This piercing chill

Emerges from my singled seclusion…

And I search for you, my partner, Just you.

You, with your warmth,

Like a midday sun at its zenith,

Dissolves the frost-forged ramparts of skepticism and encasement, By the hopeful blaze's beacon,

Oh, my beloved.

From "Songs of Passion,"

February 1988.

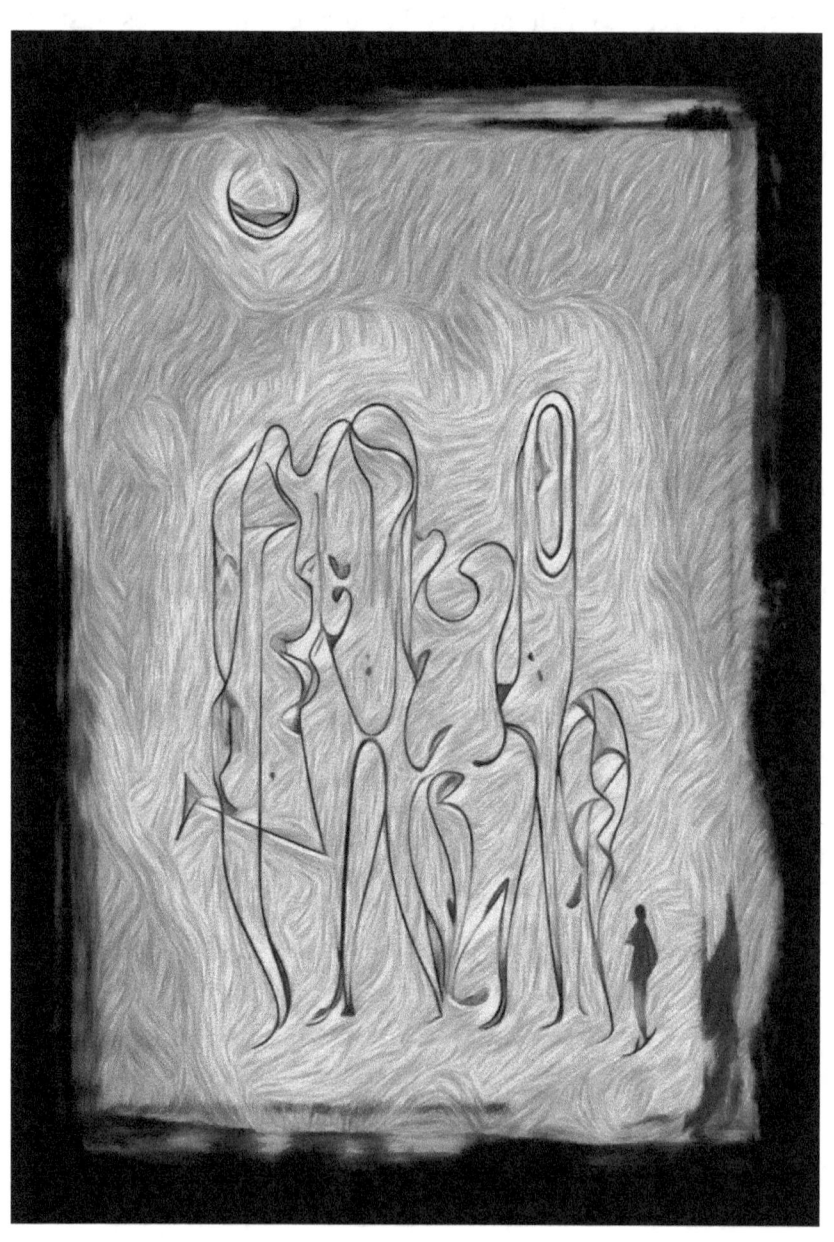

Awaiting What Comes

In the half-light, we hold expectations—soft, silent—
Time strips yesterday's visions as we sculpt unseen tomorrows.
No legacy of years clings to our flight;
We pirouette, timeless, against the dark canvas.

Not as flowers, but as unknown phenomena we emerge,
Blazing with a ferocity uncharted, undimmed.
Our love, untethered, seeks new cartographies,
We are laughter—echoing, etching mythologies anew.

Night's sentinel, the moon, stands silent;
Our wishes, spark-forged, shimmer bright.
Each stride leaves imprints glowing, ephemeral and wild,
As dawn wraps our world not in gold, but in uncaptured hues—

Every moment weaves into the unending voyage,
The rhythm of our united pulses,
Exploring the vastness of what is yet to come.

Aqua-Regia Rain

The rain drums with intensity,

mirroring the tempest within my soul.

Seated, cradling my mug,

I confront the depths of my heart—

eyes shuttered,

words teetering on the brink,

sighs billowing in my chest,

thoughts, both spoken and silent, swirl around me.

This torrent is not tears or clear water,

but aqua regia,

the sovereign dissolvent flooding my core.

A liquid that pierces, dissolving my flesh,

yet it's not sorrow's embrace—

this corrosion has no antidote,

neither in a chalice of wine,

nor in the fumes of opium,

nor in a lover's tender kiss.

Gloomy, ominous clouds release their merciless downpour,

immersing me in a caustic temperament,

transforming my roof into a colander of stories,

as my heart conceals its unspoken trials.

Phrases that many cannot grasp,

wounds etched into my heart, memories that weep.

From an arduous journey,

swiftly swept by the wind,

my heart dissolves, droplet by droplet,

along this acrid path.

I sit with a chilled cup of joe,

I sit devoid of you,

I sit alone,

without the urge to taste this bitter brew.

From the anthology "In Exile"

January 10, 2017

Arrival

She arrives,

arrayed in floral finery, steps in bloom,

each breath a soft conversation of doves aloft,

beneath skies barren of moon, where dreams linger high.

From a humble abode, aged by the elements,

she ascends,

panoramas through windows yearning for light's embrace.

Upon the sill, he stands,

awaiting the field's awakening,

murmuring to the solitude,

"Intoxicated by her approach, she comes,

clutching a star,

visions of moonlight dancing in her eyes.

Unfading, she halts time's relentless march.

Ah,

Her robes waltz in cloud-clasped grace,

twined with zephyrs, erratic in elegance;

with each step, relentless and sublime,

she draws ever nearer."

As You Exist

In your being,
clarity abounds.
With you here,
affection flourishes, and compassion weaves through our days.

While you're near,
winds dance, rains caress, storms roar,
and a sun emerges post-storm,
accompanying gazes and kisses bestowed on blossoms
strewn across fields, both far and near.

In your presence,
my eyes weave intricate dreamscapes
amongst clouds and zephyrs;
my lips, in fervor, recall you in whispers,
thoughts forever clear.

While you're with me,
paths timidly tread each night toward home's embrace,
wary of the void that lingers,
as the nightingale's call echoes your voice at my door,
carrying melodies sweeter than ever to my core.

Life unfolds in vibrant hues, a masterpiece in motion,
within my soul's desert,

your enchanting presence flows like a brook;
without you, all is but a fleeting mirage,
risen from incense smoke.

I dread to see, even fleetingly, that unkind hour
when you lie on a cold stage, dormant in slumber,
and not even the most passionate name I utter
can wake you with a smile, its warmth to lend.

No, I do not wish for this,
I cannot wish for this end.

As long as you are,
life pulses, melodies play,
and within me, a chorus of unseen birds
on each bough writhe, restless and astray.
Oh God,
I implore you, by oath, take me away
before you steal that cherished being
with your myriad ploys, sly and cunning. –

From the collection "In Exile"
August 30, 1978

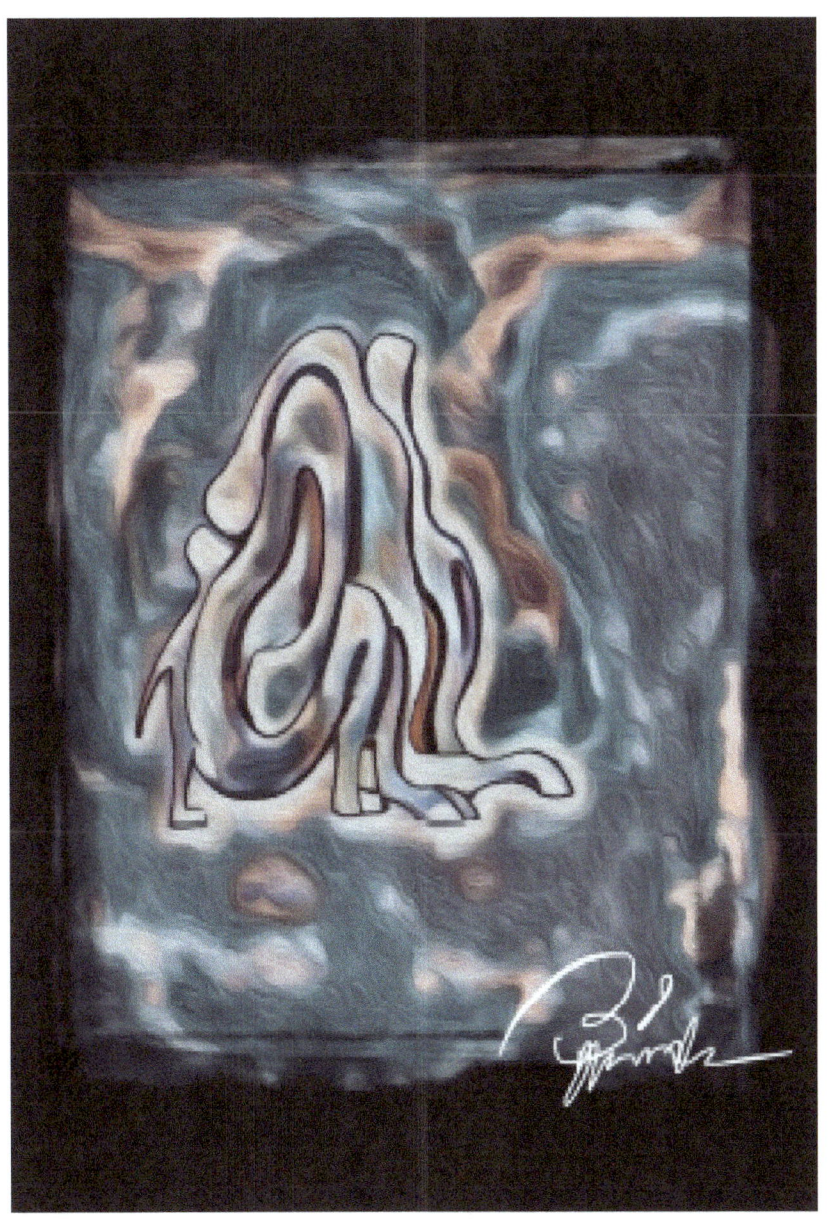

At Forty

You stand at forty where the wind,

generous, bestows forty tulips of purple grace,

only to scatter them—

yet never marring your pride,

for each petal carries a story untold.

Unyielding as ancient peaks,

you rise, head held high and dignified,

a sanctuary for leopards,

guarding their refuge against fate's plundering hand.

At forty, may your days stretch long,

your lips curve into a radiant smile,

like a garden of blossoming tulips at your feet,

each bloom a testament to your strength.

May each slumbering leopard

bloom into a cherished memory,

etched upon the hard peaks of your pride forever.

Such memories,

neither wind nor fate can pillage.

From "Songs of Passion"

May 1997, Toronto

At Sixty

Now, as you approach sixty,
oh enchanting soul,
you still seem as if you're twenty-eight,
capturing my heart and faith, just as on that first day,
with that same face and smile,
radiating sweetness and purity.

At sixty,
every line gracing your beautiful countenance
becomes a work of art,
like waves cascading one after another,
wild and intoxicated,
upon the welcoming shore of the sea;
nothing is more beautiful than that, oh endearing soul.

Together, side by side, we have traversed
through valleys and peaks,
and though at times we felt apart,
our hands, now and then,
and the belief in our hearts
held us steadfast,
calming the tumult of our journey;
we never shattered, nor did we stumble.

And I recall,

with each passing smile through the ravages of time,

how it bloomed upon your lips,

a hundredfold more resplendent than that first day,

carrying my heart with the melodies of a blossoming garden,

perfumed by thousands of flowers.

Now that you reach sixty,

do not for a moment doubt

that without you, dreams would cease to exist for me. .

Azur Stone

I sit,
weary on the porch of a home
crafted with my own hands
atop that azur stone.
I remember—
my mother, weeks after her passing,
joined the swift flight of swallows,
showing me this azur stone in a dream.
Deep in a valley,
it lies where, maybe two or three times a year—
or is it three or four—
a fierce flood washes the soil away to the sea.
My home, perched high,
became a refuge
as villagers pounded on my door during floods.

Long before I could recall,
the wind swept me away
from a wooden house my father built,
beyond the furthest memories.
My grandmother wept at the threshold,
while my mother, in her lonesome home,
remained alone with my father.
My sister, caught in the heat of the moment,
saw nothing in my departure.

My father believed

there was divine wisdom hidden

in the wind and flood that took me away one night,

crossing borders on the shoulder of the wind,

as people did in the Stone Age.

Years came and went,

my grandmother aged and

died on a bed of remorse.

From her grief, my mother

wrote a book of poetry,

tying its pages to the feet of swallows.

The home of my father's hopes, however, was stolen by a thief.

The dread of distance in my heart

has grown mightier than memory's power.

Ah,

memories came and went,

the kindest ones packed up swiftly with my heart.

On this long, painfully distant journey,

I found and nurtured a companion,

more beautiful than a blossom,

delicate as the dream just before dawn—

whom I cherished in my soul.

A singing bird never rests easy in a cage.

A plucked flower endures but a few days,

and my heart clenched with sorrow, realizing I

crafted a cage

from the fossilized remains of my candor,

where the purity of my love was imprisoned.

This very bird, dearer than my own being,

sipped from the chalice of its form in a fleeting moment,

never imagining we would build a cage

where love would be ensnared.

Years came and went.

Loves came and went.

Pieces of me in the relentless whirr of time's wheel came and went.

And nothing remained in this garden but remorse, sighs,

and possibly three or four red roses—perhaps more.

The rest vanished without a trace.

I've built a home deep in a valley,

atop that blue stone.

People in the vast plain below see my home

nestled in the dark hollow of a cave,

though I know

I've built my home on the loftiest spot of this settlement,

right upon that blue stone.

Like a meteor illuminating the night,

it came from beyond the farthest distances

to the air of my heart.

I recognize my mother in it; I know

this blue stone is a precious shard of her essence.

I know.

I know.

From the collection "In Exile"

April 2, 1996

Azure Remembrance

Azure blue,

deeper than the deepest hue,

the clearest sky I've ever known,

unmarred by clouds above, alone.

Through its breadth, a thousand birds in blue migration have flown.

Azure, azure,

the sun, a golden sphere, gleams bright,

its light adorns the vast blue sky, unmarred, free of any blight.

I remember well, before my birth into this expanse—

from one end to the other, all was blue, an azure dance.

My mother's laughter, as she swam,

echoed in the azure pond, a harmonious psalm.

Even in death, all was draped in blue,

my partner's tears upon this earthen hue,

azure, azure.

That severed lock of hair,

carried by the wind, was blue beyond compare.

Yet what escapes my grasp, what I cannot recall,

is the color of the sky where I've lived among you all—

beneath this feast of life spread wide,

a sky's shade unknown in the chapters I've tried.

Azure, azure,

deeper than the deepest blue,

azure, my heart's eternal hue.

From the collection "In Exile"

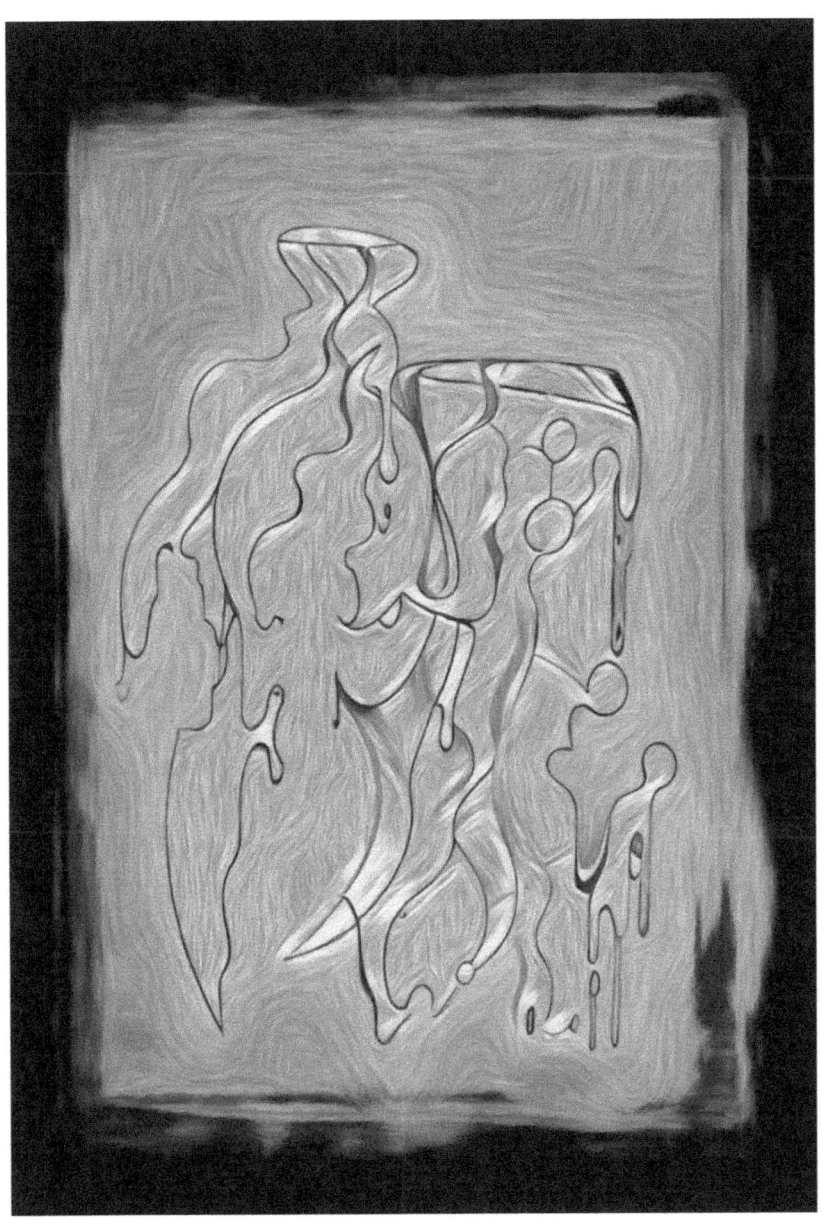

Bared Passages

Roads lie bare,

unveiled tracks declare,

desires stripped to their core, unfeigned.

As a woman released from her binds,

she embraces me firmly,

in darkness uninhibited,

mysterious as a path with no end.

These roads throb with life,

alive with intent,

tender as the clasp of a woman's arms—

yearning for my touch, soundlessly,

unbeknownst to her,

a longing that transcends comprehension.

Roads wane,

like murmurs of a tender breeze,

brushing against my being,

ushering to a secret alcove,

free of all obstructions.

I have observed roads lament in silence,

grieving for the departed, the dear ones astray,

those unacknowledged, unowned,

now dust in eternal slumber,
as hearts pine for loves afar,
crying solitary, unnoticed.

Indeed, the passages mourn.
Yet roads persist,
resembling love's own face—
desires that flame and quiver,
sorrows,
recollections.

No, roads never die.

From "In Exile"
March 26, 2016

Begin the Journey

Begin,

usher in the voyage!

Can you sense the estrangement

that lingers between us,

in a gap narrower than our kisses,

half-locked in embraces,

where a single breath nurtures

two distinct emotions

within our chests?

Do you feel the bonds collapsing,

ancient scrolls, two millennia old,

torn apart,

as something between us

crumbles to dust?

Embark on this journey; let it commence!

How swiftly the crossroads unfold their wings,

casting off the weight of fleeting moments

with a painful yearning unburdened—

the longing to separate,

to tread our paths,

to truly experience.

Do you not reckon the time for travel is now?

We must learn from the cosmos;
after an explosive burst,
its cocoon of galaxies shattered—
the universe set forth,
dust of experiences forged into life.

Initiate the trek,
begin the sojourn.

From "In Longing for Flight"
2/1364 - Tehran

Blank Page

In the darkest hour of night,
I caress the empty page,
fingertips gliding,
bestowing soft kisses,
whispering sorrows
onto its dormant surface.

It, veiled and captivated,
polishes my longing,
as beneath the moon's sweet radiance,
my words, like melting cries,
engrave dark trails on its purity.

In these desolate nights,
moments unfold upon its frame,
indulging in innocent passions,
forbidden yet tender.

Oh, beloved canvas,
forever shall I cherish your embrace,
beneath the moon's luminous glow,
where desires leave silver marks
upon my heart.

Birth

I emerge from rooftops of sorrow,

and the depths of sorrow that dwell within.

You rise from the radiant heart's depths,

imprisoned yet holding a taste of hope.

From these rooftops,

where whispers of the departed linger,

from the heights of trembling gallows,

and the lament of mist-covered roofs,

I arrive, mourning the loss of moonlight.

I understand—

your hands seek the lost corners of the soul.

Tell me of your hands' birth,

and the melancholy they carry,

for they find no solace in solitude.

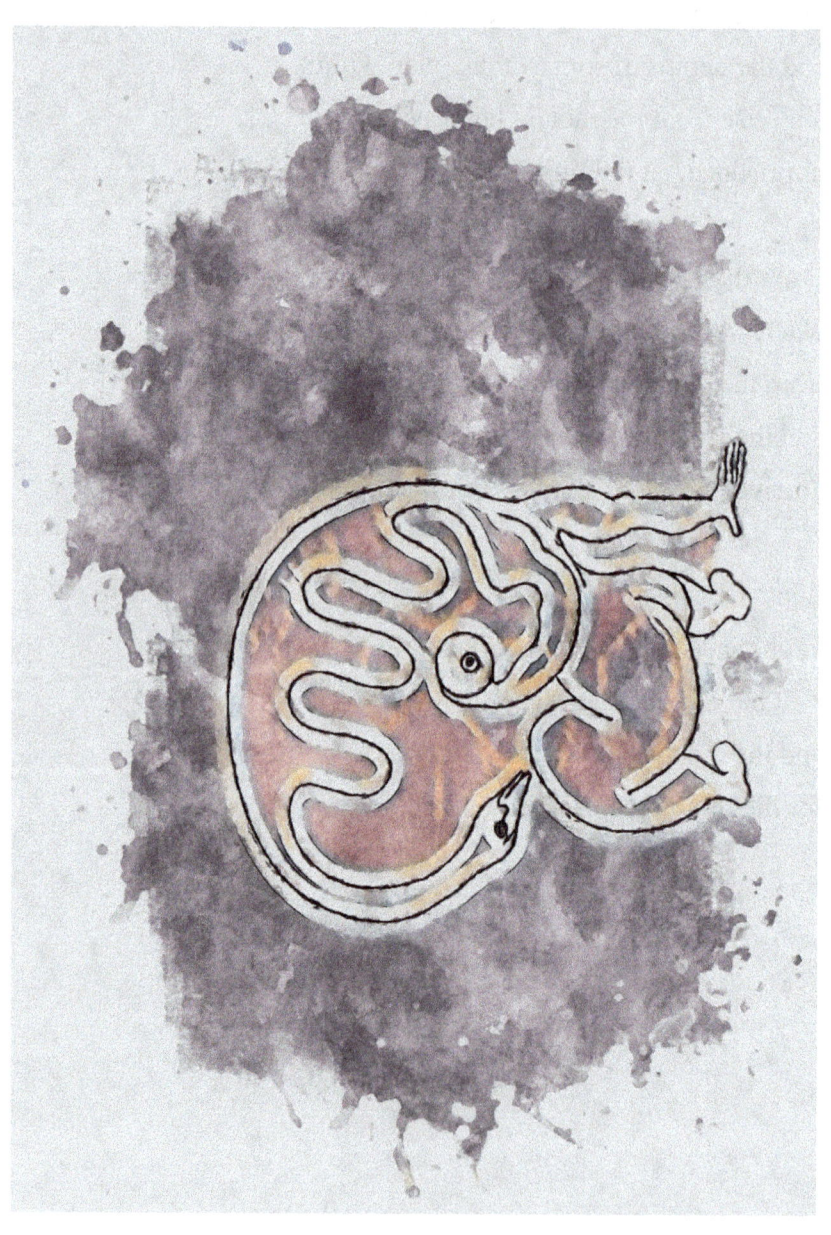

Carbon's Symphony

Within Earth's core, carbon's symphony unfolds,

a melody of emotions deep within your soul.

Connected to the shimmering stars above,

night's secrets dwell in the depths of your gaze.

At daybreak's dawn,

I've witnessed a thirsty tongue,

rolling like a current in the desert,

longing for a mirage, elusive but never near.

Oh, innocent being,

a clot of life's essence,

the monthly rhythm that women endure,

a dance of creation, yet denied the joy of birth—

how it stings—what thoughts weave through your fragile mind?

Behold!

The sunset spills its breathtaking hue,

traces of desires, bold and true,

a mother's shadow, veiled and kind,

planting seeds of hope in passersby's hearts.

Oh, child unseen, yet so divine,

a whisper of dreams that intertwine,

in the quiet of night, where longing takes its flight,

like stardust scattered across the velvet night.

******

Oh, child unseen, yet so divine...

Cavalier

Bound by the tempest's command, a fist coiled tight,

A torrent of crimson spills from unseen springs,

Burdened by scorn that clings like shadows to kin—

Not merely a man, but a rider in the night,

Within custom's grasp, heart scarred, a chest of thorns,

And a steed that charges forth through the clash of blades.

Alas, to a realm now forsaken, he has flown.

This warrior, forged in form, his vow unbroken,

Silent still against the foe's unformed claim,

To reclaim the sigh from his heart, each breath a token,

Among the fallen, framed in the battlefield's shame.

A rider in pursuit, a lance has pierced his shoulder,

Bathed in blood, yet his spirit remains unyielded,

Not just a rider, but a lover's fierce embrace,

Ever mounted on the steed of undying hope.

In the face of defeat, he casts aside

Both horse and heart, yet clings to whispered dreams.

Amid the slain, awash in the flow of fate,

He wanders through echoes of loss and despair,

Now from the horse, then from the heart, a trace,

Chasing shadows of love, in an endless search.

And as night descends, with stars like distant eyes,
He feels the weight of every battle fought,

From the collection "Lost in the Wind"
2000 - San Diego

Chalice

Unseasonably, autumn crashed

onto pathways, concealed behind a secret door—a sanctuary for my weary heart,

yet fleeting.

Restlessness consumed my soul, stirred by sorrow; it sank into profound musings, heavy and profound, questioning why fall arrived so soon.

Now I see,

nothing remains but the silver strands that carry echoes of laughter and warmth,

a testament to winter's chill knocking at my door.

Life, love, time, memories drift like autumn leaves, swirling away,

until another spring beckons, leaving only echoes of someone beneath the soil,

and even those echoes race away with the swift current of time.

I tell myself:

Do not sit in silence, do not dwell in sorrow; let your heart erupt.

Lift a cup from the hands of a kindred spirit and drink, for the moments left to you are few

within these ruins.

Life, love, desire, memories all dissolve like mist.

Dedicated to an old friend.

from "In Search of My Land" October 14, 2018

Before the earth embraces the memory of you.

Chills of Absence

As if my heart is heavily seized by despair,
As if it has shattered
In a silence too profound for words,
As if in one night, I lost the warmth of your embrace
Through a half-opened window
I should have never unlatched.

It's not merely as if—
For from this magnificence of sorrow, my heart staunchly denies,
But I know...
This journey has laid me to waste.
I shuddered to my soul,
Fearing the chill of an impending autumn.
From this heart, plundered by winter's thief,
I withered like a fragile sapling
On a branch struck by frostbite.

Without you, my love, the world
Feels drenched in my heart's own blood,
A mirage, icy as a phantom in the desert.

From the collection "In Exile"
December 21, 2016

Cigarette

In this land, where relentless monotony reigns,

Even the ethereal lady in the gardens waits,

Engrossed in her literary pursuits,

Savoring the enchanting spell of a cigarette,

As azure tendrils ascend from the depths of the sea.

Alas,

My rebellious spirit, steadfast and free!

Has spring indeed surrendered,

Leaving you ensnared in this desolate autumn of exile?

Companion

In sync with the ebb and flow of time, I stride,
Embracing the weight of a thousand years,
Their sorrowful melodies caress
The depths of my melancholic heart,
Mourning for countless birds,
Whose wings have been cruelly clipped.

Entwined with age-old anguish, I venture forth,
I brave the winds of uncertainty,
Yearning for a renewed gust of boundless wings
To grace our weary, battle-scarred shoulders,
Oh, cherished friend.

Distrust

Oh,
O children without refuge,
Adorned with crowns of thorny hue—
For which crime, which sin, do you bear
The cross of your torment, heavy and rare?

O heartrending children,
Tell me how I can
Catch hold of your little hands,
As they slip away like grains of sand,
And hold them in my sorrowful grasp,
So your rebellion may find strength to clasp
When trust is but a wisp between us.
I do not wish for this separation.
Tell me,
How can I bridge this frustration?

All that fear,
All that lack of trust,
All that distance—
A void that renders galaxies mere dust.
Behind these cold expanses,
My pitiful, sad hands, so small and meek,
Struggle to reach, yet cannot speak.

If only I could open my chest,

Cradle your little hands—

Freer from my world, a cherished guest—

In my hold, squeezing tight,

Carrying them through layers of night,

So you might see on my heart's wall,

Apart from your love,

There's nothing at all.

My strong shoulders

Bend beneath distrust's weight,

Like a fruitful tree weathering fate.

My tongue,

Like a bird trapped in a cage,

Does not sing

A song for anyone's heart—no sage.

Distrust

Is a black hole, opening wide,

Leaving nothing in its wake,

A steadfast heart that cannot glide.

Distrust, a wound

That mars time on every side,

Transforming memories,

Where hope can hide.

If only I could

Place your delicate weight upon my shoulders

And take you to visit vast plains

Far beyond your hands,

Where you might see how small the strife

Of everyday burdens, in the light of life,

In the face of a being who is you,

In the glow of pure trust—

In yourself and in me,

In all that's true.

If only I could,

Like in days of yore,

When your little hands rested, calm, in mine,

With stories shared,

With innocent and simple white lies,

Or an afternoon stroll,

I would show you the delightful smile

You once wore,

And now have lost,

Filling your heart for a while.

Oh,

If only I could do it once,

Just once.

Divine Abandonment

In the sacred orchard of affections deep,
Where emotions, like ancient trees, rise tall and steep,
His love for you, like a river, flowed without bound,
Yet his trust in you was the deepest root in the ground.

In the twilight of sorrow, he released you to the stars,
Hoping you'd navigate beyond your scars,
For he knew, in the vast cosmos of the soul,
Galaxies shimmered within you, eager to unroll.

His departure, not an eclipse but a cosmic dance,
An invitation for your spirit to take a chance.
For in the void of the infinite, he foresaw,
You revealing universes you never thought you'd draw.

Dream and Reality

Sleep is not an escape from reality,
Nor is it lured by the sweet promise of dreams.
It's not consciousness that lulls us to slumber,
But rather, sleep itself—endlessly cascading,
A tempest of wakefulness, like unbounded waves,
Colliding, intertwining into rings of hate and love,
Carrying their unsung longing to distant shores.

Sleep,
Though more terrifying than anything faced awake,
Offers a breath of release,
A yearning for those fleeting moments
Of leaving, breaking, releasing.
Sleep elevates the spirit, maligned in awareness,
Deceived and deceiving,
Those who should have been embraced.

Sometimes I ponder,
Is wakefulness merely the continuation of a nightmare,
Forgotten upon rising?
That consciousness serves as recompense for dreams
That steal me away
To a distant land where father resides,
Where mother dwells,
And my hands reach out in search of those

Who would take me in their embrace.

Sometimes I muse,

Wakefulness is the silent weeping of a soul,

Whose dreams stir to frantic screams.

Yet death embodies the beauty of a dream unchased by wakefulness,

And life—

Half dream, half awakening,

The spirit's quest for return.

Life remains as unshed tears

In the eyes of you and me,

And death resembles the oysters

That transform every teardrop

Into a star upon the dreaming horizon,

Taking you with it

Through the winding corridors of a dream

That grants you release night after night.

From the collection "In Exile"

December 14, 2016

Dew's Ballad

O verdant expanse,

Will you guide me to the dew's celebration at this dark night's end?

"What seek you on this plain, O wayward child?

You've disturbed my sweet silence tonight. If you've come to meet the sky's tears, linger a while longer.

Before dawn plants her touch on these fields, you'll see the tiny stars

resting on my shoulder,

though your boat of dreams will soon drift to distant shores,

to lands where white swans and fish await, and apples of delight hang,

suspended along drooping boughs."

I thirst, O crimson bloom! From afar, I've journeyed here.

Will you offer a bowl brimmed with dew, a moment's respite upon this land?

"I have no patience for company.

What desire do you seek, O night-wandering child?

Dew on my skin glimmers with blood and stars. With your drowsy eyes,

you won't wish to drink from the heart; leave me to my repose."

Then let me touch, O playful steed, your disheveled mane,

for the dew upon it is a silversmith of myriad dreams.

"Release my tousled mane,

O child asleep in the foothills green! Others await me on this mountain range, wide awake from ridge to ridge,

one hand grasping my mane and one clutching a gun, amidst the toppled tulips,

red tulips blooming

on the graves of the fallen."

Yet as the dawn beckons, with its soft, golden glow,

I carry the whispers of the night, where dreams and longing flow.

I, the wayward child awake on the hills!

From "In the Aspiration of Flight"

Karachi - July 1987

Duality's Dance

In night's deep embrace, I awaken alone,
Haunted by visions of a shadow well-known.
From the cosmos' vastness to life's fleeting speck,
The dance of duality leaves its subtle effect.

Abyssal depths within my soul do reside,
Where light and dark in tandem abide.
The waves of existence, they ebb and they flow,
Their dance whispers secrets that few come to know.

Beneath tranquil waters, fierce currents run deep,
While in silent meadows, restless shadows creep.
Each star in the sky, with its shimmer so bright,
Is tethered to darkness—its absence, the night.

In the heart of the forest, where sunlight does play,
Night's whispered secrets linger not far away.
A door stands between the known and concealed,
Guarding the mysteries time has yet to reveal.

Two dice of existence in Fate's hands do roll,
Representing forces that shape every soul.
One seeks the sunlight, warm and profound,
The other is drawn by the night's haunting sound.

A black hole lurks within, intentions unclear,
Mirroring a self that is held deeply in fear.
Yet, in its fierce gaze, a reflection I see,
Of the very duality residing in me.

The unity of opposites, nature's grand design,
Where every end begins, and shadows entwine.
In this cosmic dance, as ancient as skies,
The essence of duality forever lies.

Echoes of Silence

Above, if nothing else,

But the quietude of sky exists;

No ear attuned to hear your cry,

No anxious eye to witness your distress,

No heart within one's chest

To weep

Over torments beyond measure;

And shed tears for the naive spirits of a countless throng,

Who come,

Weep,

Laugh,

And perish,

With hands of yearning and envy,

Reaching toward the hushed heavens in tremor.

Yet, if upon this Earth there's naught

But the downpour of comrades' tears;

No affection remaining in the heart,

No anger slumbering in clenched fists,

No lover so passionate

To let out a shout,

Nor any stalwart shoulders left on Earth

To lean upon for support.

If nothing persists upon this Earth, indeed,

But boundless anguish

That scorches the core of your being,

Like a furnace's fervent heat;

In the depths, however,

Beneath mounds of clay and silt,

Restless dead,

Bound sleepers,

For you and me—

They claw upon bony cheeks,

And weep,

And weep,

In a damp silence

Where they lie eternally asleep.

From the collection "In Exile"

January 8, 2017

Elegy

Beloved,

I sense my final breath, shrouded in disbelief,

Eyes heavy with fear,

Gazing upon your pale, weary face.

Ruined, indeed, by dread,

Not merely for death's cruel grip that holds me fast,

But for the thought of leaving you too soon.

Departing without consent,

Without pondering the fate that awaits you,

Will you find solace, my love,

Cradled in a gentle heart, as tears fall like rain?

Elusive Elixir

Oh, how I wish to carry your beautiful face each night,

to drift through dreams,

where shadows whisper of longing,

as my heart burns in sorrow and fever from your absence.

In the embrace of sleep, I seek the kiss,

a fleeting remedy, an elixir of a thousand loves,

or perhaps a haunting echo of what was never mine.

From the collection "In Exile"

June 21, 2017

Elusive Silence

Silence does not dwell here—observe,

my eyes converse, unvoiced yet profound,

weaving tales of our shared existence in a language of silence.

Silence is not a void—witness,

my words transcend sound,

drifting to you like butterflies on the breeze.

Each glance etches stories across the canvas of your soul,

more expressive than the silence of endless fields.

There is no true silence;

the spoken and unspoken lay bare,

intertwined in this tapestry of memories,

where the same furrows and folds trace

the contours of both our faces.

From the collection "In Exile"

2017

Embers

The sun, a paramour of the moon,

And the earth, entwined in ardor for the sun,

With the moon, a cherished companion to the earth.

The sun, aflame in silent torment,

The moon, in her own hushed ascent, tinged with ash,

While the earth cradles a love profound,

That blazes as fiercely as the sun's core,

And ignites the erupting volcanoes.

Yet, humanity, born of fervent desire,

Is but a flicker,

Soon to be consumed by the raging storm of their own tears.

January 1986

Embers in the Rain

Drops whisper upon sprouts new-born,

And I, in the hush, I lay.

Dawn's white verse chants

Behind curtains of recurrence,

Stirring memories awake,

While I, swathed in gloom.

All,

All within me is ablaze,

Scorching this restless soul through.

Moist wrath entwined with sorrow,

In the guise of bleeding words,

A melody rises, like a seething ocean squall,

Stolen from this deserted shore—

Upon my lips,

Within my heart, it pales.

Night,

Draped in the heftiness of its own night,

Heart-frayed, restive,

In the flickering unrest of a lantern lost

Upon the silhouette of earth.

Night,

Deeply enshrouded in night.

Toronto - March 30, 1989

Entirety of My Life

My entire life,

a delicate perception,

vanished with your departure from my heart,

abandoning me

in the quivering shadow of a translucent bubble.

My entire life

is colorless dew,

rising with a sigh at the sun's embrace,

mingling with thousands of memories,

transforming into a raindrop,

lingering in the corner of my eye.

My entire life, my sole delight,

is the pursuit of that subtle understanding,

where the sweetness of dying intertwines

with the sharpness of existence,

echoing endlessly.

From the collection "In Search of My Land"
February 24, 2003

Enamored

The wind whispers, the wind whispers,
carrying whispers to distant realms;
how I wish to dwell in the winds,
where mountains greet the meadow,
poetry entwined with hope,
and love lingers at the end of days.

In the caress of your kisses upon the earth,
wherever you have blossomed,
the winds gently trace the contours of your form.
I long to exist within a rolling breeze,
in brief zephyrs,
as your woven essence becomes my passage.

I'd traverse through you,
a sack of childhood sorrows and joys,
leaving behind, in the damp particles of air,
the somber scent of cherished memories.
How I wish to live,
joyously in the dance of your hair,
singing with the winds the most stirring of tunes—
the song of love,
the song of verdure,
the song of the final breath.

A melody only my body and your gliding figure comprehend,
like the cool sensation of a fish through water.
The wind whispers, the wind whispers,
imploring the heart of the waves
to echo my bliss as I glide over your form.

Oh, how I wished to steal you away,
this intricate crystal lattice,
and bear you to a realm afar.
Years arrive, years fade,
carrying all to lands far,
ever so far away.

From the collection "Songs of Passion"
Tehran – May 1985

\

Entwined Essence

We are convergent specks, intricately interlaced,
From the farthest galaxies, I've traced your breath's scent.
A scent that summons me, shapes my every form,
Defining my trajectory through spaces vast and warm.

From distances so great, where light dares not to tread,
Your laughter bridges gaps in the darkest nights I've led.
On cold nights, where diamonds from my tears take birth,
I feel the warmth of you, the unparalleled glow of your hearth.

Without you, I felt cold, though never truly apart,
For you've always been there, entwined within my heart.
My frozen state arose from an absence, quite profound,
A distance not of space, but where our souls are bound.

I yearn to be with you, beside, within, complete,
A tiny fragment of your vastness, in love's rhythm, our hearts beat.
To be what you desire, to resonate with your call,
In this intricate dance, you are my all.

Oh, love, so intertwined with the essence of me,
Forever connected, as vast as the sea.

Eternal inquiry

Anyone can stretch out their arms,

Climb up, bit by bit,

Aiming for the big leap,

Pause and scope out the depth below.

Anyone can pull off a dramatic escape,

So you'd stare, eyes wide, jaw dropped,

Worried they'd crash and die.

But who possesses the audacity?

Tell me, alongside me,

Who truly possesses it?

After all that intense build-up,

Who'd jump from a height greater than their own courage,

Letting go, diving into the waves,

And truly breaking free?

This is the essence,

The eternal inquiry,

And forever will it be.

Envy

Do not scold, my love, in anger's fiery blaze,

For bitterness will only deepen love's dark haze.

This heart, once tossed from frown to frown's cruel domain,

Now heals, regret—a balm to soothe the pain.

Enhancing Voice

Her voice, like a gentle breeze, whispered without a bound,
Carrying dreams and hopes in every note it found.
Every word she sang, a story to astound,
Weaving emotions, like threads, tightly wound.
Her presence, a symphony in chaos,
Her enchanting verses, like precious gems unfurled.

And she embraced
The rawness of life in every tender touch,
Her love, a flame that burned, oh so much.
Her arms, a sanctuary where sorrows would clutch,
Transforming them into strength with a gentle brush.
In her embrace, I found solace and peace,
A refuge from darkness, a sweet release.

And she became
The muse that inspired, a creative fire,
Igniting passion, making hearts aspire.
Her words, like poetry, set souls afire,
Guiding us through depths, higher and higher.
In her presence, we found inspiration anew,
A beacon of light in a world so askew.

And she enchanted
With her verses, woven with art,

Speaking truths that touched the deepest part.
Her enchantment, like a spell, captured the heart,
Leaving a lasting imprint, like a timeless work of art.
In her enchantment, we found solace and delight,
A gift to cherish in every day and every night.

Enchantment

She arrived,

on this night's pinnacle, wakeful until dawn's light,

her skin billows with the ocean's pulse.

Deep within her bosom, she submerged her grief—

it gyrated there,

sending out the muted reverberations of the lost,

echoing through her longing's abyss.

Her lips, a misty nebula,

her tears dance in the orbits of her eyes;

her mirth, elusive as a slippery fish,

her sobs rise like a vast, fathomless tide.

In her heart's secret hollows, she harbored

an impatient conch,

Urging to distill pearls from humanity's shared convictions.

She stepped,

into my realm of skepticism,

moving to a cadence that sculpted sorrow itself,

a symphony of yearning and loss,

drawing me into her depths...

From the collection "Songs of Enchantment"
September 1987 – Karachi

Existence

I am not,

Not so alive that I am ensnared

by the murmur of a mere word,

Nor so deceased

to settle into the silence of memory's bed.

I am not,

As I am,

A stone swept along the river's bosom,

Caught in the swift caress of waves,

Before your gaze of beauty,

Liberating it amidst the water's roaring swell.

I am not

Except the wave that rises,

Bestowing coolness upon my being

As it kisses the crystal of your stems,

Anticipating your stone's throw upon the stream,

Embracing my formless self.

I am not

But a glowing ember of light,

Passing through the sphere of your eyes,

Guiding you to tumultuous undulations,

With faint echoes of memories,

Waves,

And images—vivid and void,

Eternally etched by the throw of stones.

I am not

But a fleeting ray of thought,

Transiting your physical crystal,

Fragmenting and merging,

Capturing, weightless and dissonant,

Particles of being and of my own non-existence.

You seek me in the grains of my essence;

My being exists,

And all that has been marked by my presence

Or whatever binds with you.

My non-being,

My death,

The eternity where I found peace,

You will stir to greater turbulence.

Ah,

Caster of stones upon my being's pond,

I wish to share my non-existence,

The raw moments of my death,

As I draw away from the beauty of your stems.

So you might see in each grain of my being

Thousands of annihilated particles hidden deep.

I long to carry

The stones your beautiful eyes seek

From the depths of the river flowing over my grave,

So you might discover that in the memory of each wave,

Formed by the leaping of stones,

Multitudes remain concealed.

I am not,

I am not,

Not so alive

As to find solace in your embrace,

Nor so deceased

As to be forgotten on the shoulder of a wave.

From "In Exile"

November 20, 2016

Father

If there stands a verdant tree upon the ground,
I know its roots have run across my father's shoulders.

At times, I muse;
it's time to rise,
to trace with eyes and hands
the soil of every threshold, every alley
he has walked,
to carve a path for witnessing his essence,
to embrace him,
and express:
"How deep the envy of memories."

And weep wholeheartedly,
so he may see the void,
befriended by my soul in his absence.

If in the sky's bosom there still dances
a path among the stars,
I know a nest is cradled in my father's palms.

And I,
I've built my home upon the crest of waves,
on the shoulders of the wind's every whim,
and sat without him—

anxious, heartsick, dulled,

in this wounding estrangement.

Words abound.

The yearning for unspoken words

within me is just as vast,

and father is no more.

In my stillness, his essence blooms

like night-blooming cereus in the cracks of my heart.

From the collection "In Exile"

May 2016

Father's Remembrance

Forty days since my father left
this arid soil, burdened by hardship, barren and bare.
Forty nights I have wandered,
he, unfettered, winged,
hovering above the valleys of my heart, fraught with yearning—
Alas!

Words clamored in my chest,
holding hope that perhaps one day
I might speak to him,
of the sorrow of this fatherless journey
that charred me through.
I know,
with my heart as witness, that he too harbored
a trove of tales untold.

Though he has passed, until that day
at the appointed hour when I
shall follow in his wake,
pining for that fleeting moment,
forever elusive,
I burn within this inferno of grief.

My heart, awash with tears,
craves just a glimpse of him.

From the collection "Lost in the Wind"
September 2003, San Diego

Farewell

Depart, my friend,

unto tomorrow,

to wherever your journeys may lead.

Do not flee from love,

nor tremble at the battle—

travel with two confidants:

your patient heart of lava stone, and my wounded own,

with a rose placed in between.

Go forth, dear companion,

farewell on your voyage,

awaiting another dawn.

From the collection "Arias of Fervor"

July 1987, Karachi

Faded Moon

O Moon,

O beloved, beguiling jewel of night,

Valiant faces laid upon the earth seek you,

Prisoners casting hopeful eyes

Upon the gallows' stark silhouette.

O Moon,

Radiant orb of soft luminescence,

Through shadowed cells devoid of dawn's embrace,

Why do you pale tonight,

Mute, absent the tar's haunting melody,

More silent than last night's vigil?

Your ashen cheeks, dear Moon,

Capture the eve's deep gloom;

Speak, utter a whisper,

Lest the heavens veil their view

In dense clouds, fevered and dark.

Cry out, if only to pierce silence's weight.

"Leave me be; what is it you seek?

This night you unfurl my solitude with disquiet."

Thus the cold Moon spoke to me.

"Let him be,

With a heart weary and bleeding,

He shall compose verses tonight,

Verses he cares not for others to hear."

Thus the fierce wind spoke to me.

For God's sake, speak,

Say something!

And the Moon cast its sullen ash

Over hills and rippling brooks,

Scattering shadows upon doors and walls,

Drizzling on ponds and riderless plains,

Hymning a song we'll never wish to hear,

In sleep nor wake,

Bereft of awareness.

Color drained from the Moon beyond the horizon,

Fading and dissolving,

Journeying into silence.

From the collection "In Exile"

September 20, 2016

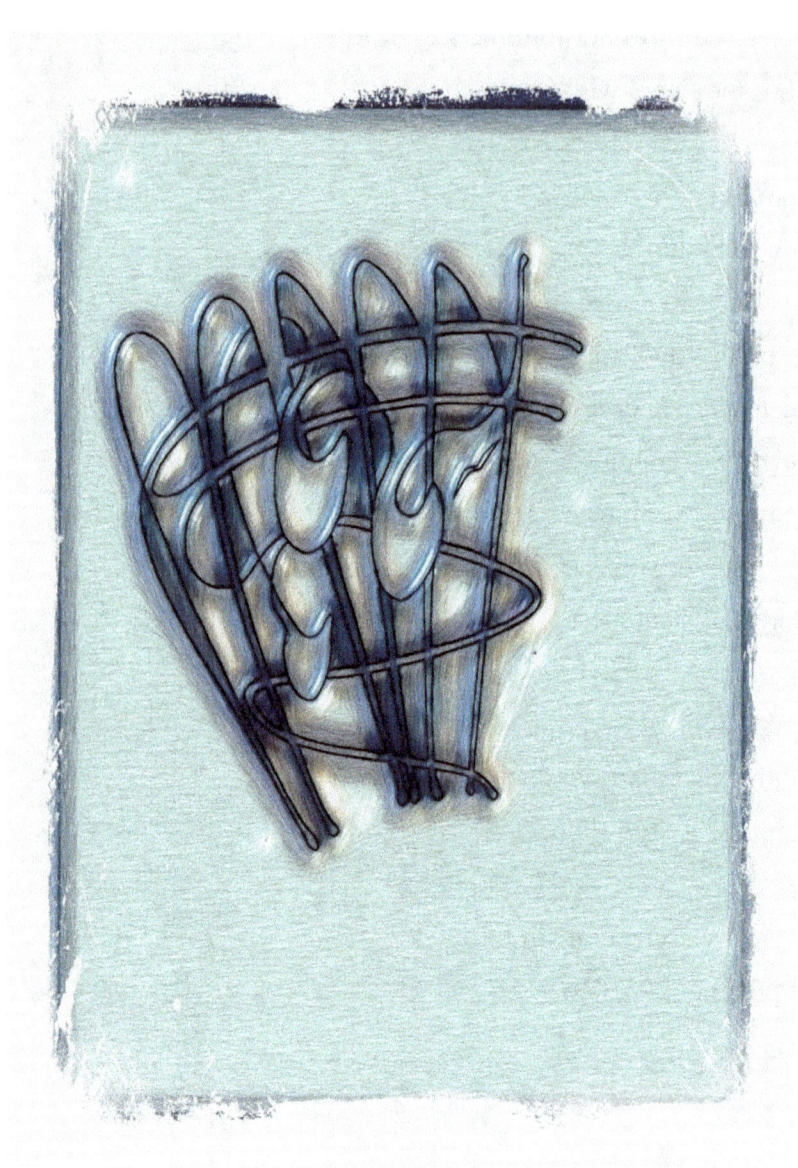

Fear Not

My strength was vast, beyond measure,

And so was my love,

Yet I couldn't release you,

Couldn't free myself

In my solitary retreat.

In that harmony of soul and heart

That yearned for you,

Those moments craving

To be within you,

I found my capacity

And my liberation.

And now,

That love is no longer mine,

As if it never was,

Those enchanting moments lost.

Oh, if only my heart would settle,

This naïve heart of mine,

In blood by a dagger's strike.

O hand, fear not!

Grasp a blade,

Sharper than the traitor-friend's unkind dagger,

And free my sorrowful heart.

O hand,

Fear not,

Rise in complicity with the friend's knife.

"Lost in the Wind"

August 2003 - San Diego

Flaws

Should I morph into a fish that glides below,

I'd find myself ensnared, a spectacle on show.

Or if I became a bird, roofing the skies,

In the air, stones thrown, my freedom belies.

Or suppose I turned deaf, blind, and mute,

Or even passed away, still they'd find fault,

Enough said in their own way,

Thus, I harbor no fear from any soul's rebuke;

Let them cast their blemishes; I will not be shaken.

Flood of Memories

Night,

I summon the essence of that eve,

Within the garden's embrace, together we thrived,

Where the verdant moisture of life

Struck roots through my very skin.

Ah,

How have you let it slip from memory,

Your wishes to bloom across me,

Branches laden with deep red petals,

From my womb's shadows,

A child unfurling toward the gleam of a lantern.

A child with a smile fresh as jasmine,

Lips that rival the buds of red roses,

Legs embedded strong like stems in the earth,

Eyes brimming with the buzz of myriad bees—

This child, a child

Whose destiny mirrors autumn's resolve,

Obstinate as the evergreen's verdure,

Among countless limbs, anticipant buds stir.

Of that night,

Of that moment's insistent narrowness,

I recount the genesis of this torrent,

Blessed upon lovers, an omen,
To myriad wombs, its pledge intertwined.

From the collection "Songs of Passion"
June 1988 – Toronto

From Ashes to Hope

What rests entombed within the earth
shall sprout anew,
whether a seed of verdant growth,
Evolving into sheaves of wheat, a shrub, or a sprawling tree,
a fragment of bread, a chalice of wine,
or the elation of mirth.

Or if it takes the guise of metal,
transforming into the skeletal frame of a structure,
within the grip of a mighty spade,
or fused with a weighty mallet,
or molding itself into a leaden bullet,
shattering humanity's aspirations into ruins.

Should it manifest as a droplet of water,
quenched by the parched soil,
it shall surge forth once more from the ground,
whispering ceaselessly within the veins of a spring.

Thus, let us believe in all that is sown in the earth,
faith in our departed brethren,
with bodies bruised,
chests rent asunder,
hearts impaled by daggers,
Yet pride standing tall.

Let us hold faith for those whose names

and ivory pride

remain unremembered upon their bloodied beds.

May the sacred fury of your departed kin

dance upon wooden gallows for the crime of love,

or clamor in a corner against death,

before the command of "Fire" spills their blood upon the ground,

All anonymous and enamored with their people.

Allow your departed ones,

who slumber within the soil with unfulfilled desires,

those who danced with you,

and before you, to the rhythm of scarlet roses,

emerge from earth and icy ashes,

within your footsteps and through your songs.

And in the end,

have faith

that your departed do not perish;

they shall dwell beside you,

as you strive for the sun,

to bring its radiance down.

Retain your belief in the fallen,

those who cultivated rain, seeds, and metal within themselves, for the day of recompense.

June 1985

Frozen Veil Sonnet

Frost's intricate etchings, my being implores,

Icy lattice embraces, leaves me sightless, encore.

Like a lost comet, adrift in the dark,

No scintillate sun, just void that embarks.

Under winter's weight, where whispers bind,

Years exposed to biting cold, unkind.

Why linger here, in this foggy abyss,

When life's vibrant moments I sorely miss?

In solitude's chamber, where walls close in,

Beneath pallor's veil, I wear thin.

Brittle, I fracture in the hoarfrost's scripts;

Shrouds entwine as my aspiration slips.

Winter's tenure, relentless, strips my warmth;

Conviction fades, ensnared by the cold's grasp.

Gambler

Beside the heart, a harbor dark and deep,
A lantern's glow, the moonlight's gentle sweep.
Hooves of the waves, like horses in their stride,
Their foamy manes tossed by the wind with pride—
They toss the wandering heart astray.

Waves clash fiercely, against the rocks they fight,
Eroding trust, a fleeting hold on sight.
Wave upon wave, time's fluid dance unfolds
On fossilized coral rocks, where turmoil molds.

A gambler unmatched, in games of chance delight,
With dice and cards, he played through day and night,
The Ace of Hearts on the horizon's wall he threw.

Oh, sleepless Queen of Spades, desired and sought,
The bride of dreams, a key to a small abode.
A night of joy in trust's deep embrace,
Your breath's warmth, his weary heart did chase.
Yet bitterness of exile, his body tasted true,
Upon the water's surface, he floated through.

I roll the dice upon the ground, I see
One and one, a pair of loneliness it be.

"Ah,

O restless Queen of Spades,

Grant me the key to your heart's hidden glades.

Trust the horizon that breaks my bones,

And to my boat, sailing towards love's zones."

Ghoul

I know not if there exists someone
who does not seek an ancient lamp in this world,
a flickering flame, an old lantern,
where a solitary, cold-hearted, half-dead ghoul
remains trapped, still bound.

I know not if, at this moment,
one exists who knows not foolishness,
who would not endure the slightest hardship
to ignite a worn-out lantern of bygone eras,
and deliver them,
in hope that such a ghoul may conjure
hidden desires.

A ghoul awaits,
shrouded in smoke, dark and murky,
taking form in an instant,
face to face.

Such a man,
his entire life filled with thorns and toil,
still carries countless hidden desires within,
each one a thorn piercing his soul.

This is a suffering man,

who, beside a bloodstained bread in his heart,

also had cheese on his table,

on a cold, wintry night,

beside his worn-out lantern,

not a mere light, but a centuries-old extinguished hearth,

his hands futilely warming them.

Under his breath, he mournfully sings:

"Oh hearth, once warm and kind,

with my hands,

now silent,

cold and lifeless like my heart,

broken in this wretchedness and solitude.

You are not with me, even for a moment, tenderly,

and I am left without you,

neither with this bright hearth,

nor with the hearth that offered refuge in this fire,

on a cold night when my heart froze like stone."

And in that moment of despair,

when he had no hope left in anyone,

in the unbelieving astonishment of his eyes,

it seemed as though a breath of smoke escaped

from the shattered ice and vanished into darkness,

revealing a majestic presence.

Indeed, a wondrous ghoul came forth,

not a mere figment of imagination or illusion.

The man, upon seeing the ghoul,

was filled with longing and hope for their union.

He half-rose and sat up,

"Oh alas, he had no breath left in him,

nor madness in his mind,

for he had used it all up in his tears of joy."

Though it took him a while to understand in his heart,

the accusation that seemed unbelievable,

the ghoul had come to spill his blood.

The bewildered man, however,

had no time left,

no hesitation or hope left in him,

nor the ability to run away,

to save himself from this deadly fate.

The last temptation before death,

that which belongs to no one,

neither fear nor desire,

attacked him.

The ghoul said to him:

"Until this night reaches dawn,

you have plenty of time to kill me,

and I ask this of you,

tell me,

what sin have I committed

that death is my punishment for your freedom?"

Although the ghoul had the desire to accuse,
he inclined towards conversation.
The man had no urgency
to inquire about the anger and resentment
that the ghoul had hidden within;
he asked with caution:

"For three thousand nights,
I have been trapped in my silent home,
such was the longing for freedom in me,
that I promised my heart,
to anyone who would save me,
I would give half of the earth's treasure and all the wealth of the
sea,
in the solitude of my windowless room,
my eyes anxiously focused
on the tightly closed door.
Oh alas, no one was found,
and no one knocked on the door."

The ghoul poured out his anger;
the man remained silent.

"Although I was
so tightly bound,

I could hear your conversations and laughter,

the venom of envy

pierced my heart,

the stories of your love that came with every storm and wind,

my eyes remained vigilant,

not for a year, not for ten, but for a thousand."

Laughter came to the lips of the monster,

not of joy, but bitter.

Tears came to the man's eyes.

"With my heart in chains,

I vowed that if someone comes to save me,

I will be their servant for life,

with a ring in my ear.

And he never sees, at any time,

a wish that doesn't come true.

I made promises with my heart,

and it turned out that years passed,

year after year,

not just one or ten, but thousands.

Oh, alas,

not a spring,

nor an autumn,

nor the wine of rain

poured onto my burnt heart in this torment and fear."

"Let me tell you a short story;

there is no way until dawn.

Such anger and turmoil poured into my heart

that I said to myself,

I no longer have a desire for salvation.

I have no longing to see anyone in my mind,

who comes to me so late,

and in this dilemma of fear that settled in my heart,

that someone comes,

hoping to take my revenge someday,

without asking what happened to me,

with a tired body and a beard,

or what I desire.

I made a pact with my heart,

to deserve this delayed arrival,

to take my sweet soul from him,

with a pain that no one in this world has seen."

The man said, "I have no words, save my soul.

My soul is not sweet,

my soul is pain and torment, no more,

for it had no end."

The monster said, "If you have no desire or fear,

why do you cry?"

The man said, "You see,

the tears of blood on my weary cheeks,

it is not fear of death;

my tears were for you,

and the agony that went into your soul,

that made you think we humans,

besides happiness and love,

sought nothing for each other.

Alas, like me, in torment,

life with all its good and bad;

if this is why we humans exist,

or if we were created for others,

whose gifts are cheap in meeting."

The monster roared in anger,

"If you have something unsaid,

say it now!"

The man said, "Do not be angry for no reason;

I have little desire or words in my heart,

and if I have any fear, it is this,

that there is no desire or longing in anyone's heart,

even though it may be abandoned.

If death is the consequence,

then there is no desire or longing in anyone's heart."

Let me tell you a short story:

what we have said,

it is the story of our hearts,

the story of a monster,

imprisoned within our chests,

that whenever we approach it,

once again, this mad heart thinks,

how late we have come.

From the collection "In Exile"

30th September 2016

Grandma

Yearning for the moonbeam's embrace,

In Ahvaz's vibrant nights of blooming jasmine.

Beneath the weathered frame of grandma,

She hums and sings, her melodies carried by the wind,

Her ancient tunes, a tapestry of memories.

As the mighty body of Karun rover roars,

Nearby, by my side,

It tumbles and nourishes the ancient roots,

Hidden deep within the soil's embrace.

To breathe, to let go,

Of all the beauty and disquieting serenity,

To embrace the sorrow shadowing grandma's tomorrow.

Growth

At love's threshold,

Evergreens await the birth of rain,

Day by day, and still.

And your memory, oh, cloud,

Drifts softly, a profound melody,

Resonant like gentle dews of the breeze,

Nurturing the petals of hope.

From the collection "In the Hope of Flight"

Autumn 1982 - Tehran

Have Faith

Trust in the buried,
for from the earth's embrace,
sprouts life anew—
a grain might rise as wheat,
manifest as bush or bough's vast reach,
transform to bread's nourishment,
wine's mirthful dance,
or laughter's light.

Or when it's ore beneath the loam,
it may find form in structures' bones,
as the shovel's unfaltering hand,
a hammer's steadfast blow,
or a bullet—harbinger of lead—
tearing through the hopes of humankind.

A water drop, caressing
the parched thirst of the ground,
will whisper upward once more,
a tale that trickles through spring's eternal veins.

Place belief in what the soil cradles,
in the honored fallen—
their flesh scarred,
their torsos cleft,

their hearts impaled,

yet with dignity, standing sovereign.

Believe in nameless souls, whose alabaster virtues fade,

unrecalled upon their crimson pallets.

Watch the hallowed ire of the lost

pirouette upon the gallows, defiant,

cry out 'gainst the specter of demise,

their essence melding, unmarked, with the land

in fervent love for kin and kindred.

Imagine the silent, yearning rest of those who slumber

beneath damp earth—

they who were your comrades, moving

to the tempo of crimson blooms,

each petal a memory,

each stem a story yet untold.

Arise they do from dust and bone-chill gloom

with your step, in the echo of your hymn.

And so, accept with unwavering heart—

your perished never wane,

for they will endure beside you,

as your hands reach heavenward,

gripping the brilliance of the sun to draw it close.

Believe in those struck down,

who've sown within themselves the seeds of rain and iron,
awaiting harvest's day of truth,
where seeds and soil intertwine,
and life's eternal greens prevail.

June 1985 - Teheran

Heart of the Sea

Within my chest, the heart of the sea beats tightly,
before love pierces it with a dagger's might.

The heart of the sea beats,
as wearied as my own heart's plights,
echoing the crash of waves against the shore,
whispering the hidden yearnings evermore.

And hence,
thump,
thump,
thump—
the sea's bitterness and its melodies
float within my soul's depth,
a tornado of agony and thrill.

Hedgehog

To the extent that every passerby and acquaintance

have torn my heart with thorns,

if one day you were to rip it open,

you would find not a joyful and drunken soul,

just a sorrowful hedgehog

inside its cage's corner,

curled tight, quills raised,

a fragile fortress against the world's gaze,

yearning for warmth that never comes.

From the collection "In Exile"

November 17, 2016

Hope's Gaze

Each leaf that dances on a rose's bough,

Whispers a hope, a longing to be with you now.

Yet when a leaf descends, drifting far away,

It's the hope shattered by your deceitful sway.

Hush of Leaves

Crunch, crunch,

the whisper of leaves

as they fall upon the ground,

sharing their last secrets

in the chill of autumn,

beneath our tramps.

each echo a memory,

transformed by time into a larvae,

a reminder of what is yet to be.

Crunch, crunch,

spring arrived and departed,

tiny caterpillars nestled,

dreaming of transformation,

delicate butterflies

dying for warmth,

the promise of reclaimed life,

as hope unfurls with the blooms.

Crunch, crunch,

summer slipped by, unnoticed,

doves sang soft melodies

among green branches,

carrying your sorrow

on the wind's gentle embrace,

ignorant of the harsh fall,

the life that recycles over and over.

Crunch, crunch,

yellow leaves, orange and green,

dressed in vibrant hues,

dance upon forgotten graves,

echoes of laughter long gone,

deep memories intertwined,

loves pressed beneath the snow,

stories waiting to fade away

On the shoulder of a breeze.

Crunch, crunch,

winter will pass,

many years will follow,

yet the fallen leaves

continue to sing,

crunch, crunch,

whispering through the stillness,

beneath the steps of passersby

who do not seek your name,

nor sing of you,

the one who was my undeniable love,

for we have faded into forever,

but our whispers linger on,

woven into the fabric of soil and roots.

I am Thirty

At thirty years old,
it feels like thirty years have passed
since I fell in love.
And the scars of thirty red roses
still linger in my heart.

Oh,
you wild deer of my desires,
which cunning lion of disgrace
lurks perpetually for the veins of your passion?

And you, oh mournful fish of my pride,
after all those storms and hunts,
in whose net of destiny
will your fate be sealed?

In the refuge of every smile,
there's a teardrop
that makes its taste pregnant.

In Love with Life

Neither did God desire the heart's retreat,

nor did the heart yearn for the divine.

Joy did not settle in my chest,

nor did serenity,

nor any sense of pride.

Life flows onward,

carrying me from the day's awe

to the cold wonder of night's embrace.

In those deep, nocturnal dreams,

I wander from home to home,

seeking a single word,

a fleeting pretense—

now and then,

sweetly cuddled in the arms

of a dear one nestled

in my heart's corner,

year after year,

until I seek them in my dreams.

Life moves forward,

with all its good and ill.

From the heart's depth, sometimes I laugh;

other times, in sheer despair,

I scrape my face with my own sharp fingernails—

occasionally striking the cold,

colorless walls of indifference,

so close, yet distant.

Fists pound in restless frustration—

and there I am,

sitting with friends, many,

bringing smiles to their faces.

At times I limp alone in solitude,

away from the crowd,

to hear no news,

to spare a solitary heart

from any light's worry.

Life passes swiftly,

and I remind myself how wonderful it is,

that I have come, seen,

lived with all from dusk till dawn.

Still, I wonder,

what endures but the wind's howl in my hand

and the cloud's cry in my eye?

Though there's no fear of death in me,

life, I dearly love—

its trepidation, suffering, and torment.

In mirage I look after with thirsty lips,

seeing a beloved,

stealing a kiss, tasting the wine's bitterness;

I adore it all.

I am in love with life itself,
passionately in love.

From the collection "In Search of My Land"
21 September 2018

I Shall Write

In a land made of paper, dwelling deep in ink's swell,
words tango untethered, weavers of some wicked spell.
As night's darkness dissolves into truth's dawning light,
I'll conjure stanzas bold, in defiance of the fright.

Here, the horizon of language stretches vast,
baring hidden verities, aligning star to star.
Gentle now, the harrowing heft of our finite dance,
within these worded whispers, I find life's silent romance.

My pen roams through existence's tapestry, vibrant and vast,
plumbing love's labyrinthine depths with each inscribed contrast.
From liberty's lushness springs my unfettered script's soar,
while in death's shrouded corridors, wisdom's keys I implore.

Rhythms inscribed, silent yet throbbing with life's own charge,
my verses vault toward realms untouched, on airships large.
This untethered poem, wild, may never breach
the hollows of your hearing, nor the depths of your speech.

I Shall Pen

I shall pen,
wordlessly tuneless,
a verse into the velvet depths of night.
I'll carry it with me to realms unknown,
where worlds abound,
to where
ease flows like a gentle stream,
as effortless as a child's playful smile.

I shall inscribe a poem,
and with it journey
to lands uncharted still,
where love's embrace is untroubled,
transforming the solemn weight of death as sung
into the sweetness that lingers in a grin.

I shall write for the heart within,
melodies celebrating the unrivaled grace of being,
the aesthetics of dying,
for death is but the quiet essence of love,
originating with you,
finding in me an everlasting continuation.

Yes, I shall write,
without a word, void of melody,

and depart to dimensions unseen,

with a poem that might never reach your ear,

yet echoes in the silence,

a testament to the bond we share.

In Quietude

Allow me,

In God's gentle cradle of stillness,

To sit with you in silence and weep, without a single tear,

For a grain of sand within the oyster's keep is precious beyond measure.

Let it be,

In the brimming hush, I'll fix my gaze upon you,

Carving a path

To illuminate memories steeped in sorrow, so distant yet near.

Silence, at times, holds such sanctity

That the purity of unspoken words fades before its might,

Like the silent pulse of a harbor

That frees you from the chaos of the night.

When lips are bound to the rack,

Do not echo those words once more,

For your presence alone is a treasure,

A universe unto itself, to explore.

My friend, for the love of God,

Let not our connection fray

Over the repetition of old narratives

Or the mere utterance of phrases we say.

From the collection "Songs of Passion"

January 1990 - Toronto

In Remembrance of Ahmad

Each brother, in turn, has left my side,
Ahmad, the first, slipped away with fate's tide.
Then Mahmood, too, in silence bade goodbye,
And Yosef, earlier still, fell to a noontime's ruthless scythe.

Oh brothers, to what invisible realms have you fled?
Longings within me stir for your voices; my heart, it bled.
Remains there naught but the gentle warmth of days past,
And laughter's echoes that in dimming memory find no repast.

My brothers,
Our spring was chased away, untimely in its flight,
As autumn crept in, cloaked in the moon's cold light.
Once, horizons glimmered, burnished with our dreams gilt,
Now, their brilliance fades, and the colors dim with silt.
The expansive world narrows without your presence; it constricts,
Journeys now, lines drawn in stone, stripped of their mystics.

In death, there lies beauty,
Yet its premature knock is acknowledged with dismay.
It offers a gateway to freedoms untold,
To memories where laughter mingles with the light of day.
Yet, it came too swiftly, a thief in the night,
Leaving shadows where our shared laughter once took flight.

With Ahmad's departure,

My soul bears a grievous wound, scored deep.

Ahmad, not a luminous celestial, not star, nor sun's sheen,

He was Ahmad, a presence among men, fiercely keen.

In the chambers of affection, his spirit found home,

With tender silence, in their midst, he would roam.

With fervor, he lived, embraced life without restraint,

Departed with purpose, leaving hearts that now faint.

Ahmad, cherished above measure,

Now withdrawn from our earthly fry treasure.

Within me, my heart sobs anew,

In desolation, it grieves, through and through.

"From Faraway Places" collection

August 7, 2017

In the Shadow of Spring

Always, spring arrives alone,
Down pathways within your heart,
Where beds of hope are gently sown,
Eternally unfurled, a work of art.

And always, spring—
An insistent call draws near,
A song of longing, a desire profound,
A melody spun from the heart's own sphere,
In the path where skylarks sound.

So it is, my friend,
Spring weaves its way to us,
Demanding kisses from life anew,
To love, to let go, to trust,
Even as autumn's chill may ensue.

You may stand still, solemnly grieved,
At the grave of yet another loss,

From the collection "Lost in the Wind"
March 1997, Toronto

In This Realm

Once again, crickets serenade me,

Sparrows weave melodies just for me.

Whence do they glean my name?

In this realm, my name is unknown,

In this realm, strangers roam alone,

No trace of recognition to claim.

Perchance, a dream it seems,

To awaken would be a loss, it teems.

Could it be that in slumber's grasp,

I behold these crickets, these sparrows bold,

Whispering my name, stories untold?

In Tranquil Moments

In tranquil moments, whispers softly fade,
As nature's symphony takes the stage.
The rustling leaves in gentle breeze cascade,
Revealing secrets of this earthly page.

No need for silence's deceitful guise,
For truth abounds in melodies profound.
Each note a tale, each rhythm a surprise,
Unveiling beauty where it can be found.

Yet still, amidst the music's sweet embrace,
A yearning silence lingers in the air.
A pause, a breath, a moment's grace,
Inviting hearts to ponder and to share.

So let us cherish both the sound and hush,
For in their blend, life's wonders gently rush.

In Vigil

Behold,
witness this figure, so serene,
resting upon ancient soil.

Gaze upon this shape,
like the departed who shun my fate,
awaiting the cadence of your stride,
yearning for the day you'll tread
the path to your motherland,
woven in threads of time.

Behold this form,
take heed,
I lie motionless, hopeful,
like souls who linger,
unwilling to embrace the silence,
awaiting the call that bridges the divide.

Ink for the Verse I'll Write

Monochrome like night's deep cloak,

Fading into a dawn, asleep in haze.

A path without moon or mist, resembling

My heart suspended in the space of seeing you.

Like chessmen cast, between love and demise,

On checkered squares of black and white—

Gambled hearts, heedless of plight,

Our feelings, callously enlisted in play.

Yet gold and silver shine alike,

A noon's heat swaying into sultry dusk,

The sun's insolence reigning in skies,

The moon's grace in watershed—a virginity

Pillaged by fish, yet still the moon shines,

Desiring the heart upon the countless waters cast.

My love,

Your cheeks bear the hue of white and rose;

Each sight of you, each smile proceeding,

Ignites my being as dawn breaks on snow,

Like verses I pledge to pen

With my blood's droplets in a moonless night,

Hoping for you to arrive, to silently whisper:

"I love you," devoid of words.

I'll compose

A poem destined to flourish

Across every meadow, every plain,

Accompanied by myriad birdsong,

Proclaiming your name,

Each and every day

From the collection "In Exile",

January 6, 2017

Ink of Night

What a heart-wrenching day it was,
Till nightfall,
A salve on the day's wounds.

Such a day, so filled with sorrow's weight,
As darkness drapes its somber shroud,
With incessant waves that whisper in the breeze,
Casting upon the shore the day's forsaken shells.

Ah, what a day, what a day it was!
Now, beneath the moon's silver scar,
Where fish sway upon the dampened sands,
The night unveils its deeper hues,
Its stars aglow,
Mirrored in the blood-stained bowls of eyes.

Alas,
What a heart-wrenching day it was.
Yet here, beneath the tranquil sky,
I pause, I breathe,
Where starry ink of night runs through my veins to write.

Inner Light

I chase not distant trails of feeble light,
In night's embrace, where darkness holds its sway.
For deep within, my own internal might
Illuminates my night and day.

No external glow, my heart longs to find,
But the inner flame that burns with pure delight.
In shadows' realm, where secrets are confined,
My light shines forth, dispelling endless night.

No need for guidance from another's gleam,
For in my soul, a beacon brightly gleams.
Our hearts entwined, in harmony we beam,
A radiant force, weaving our dreams.

No longer yearning for an outside grace,
I find solace in my inner space.

Inner Voices

In the realm of whispers and muted sights,
where shadows dance, secrets ignite,
lies a scarred heart, unyielding to fears,
embracing the whispers as darkness nears.

Silence, we don't speak of it, my dear,
nor the fears that haunt and draw near.
Your heart, shattered, fragmented like glass,
each piece a story, a painful trespass.

With you, love takes on a hue so rare,
a bittersweet melody, an affair,
through scorching flames and disdain's disdain,
your heart's last fragment carries its own pain.

Oh, with you, pain becomes strangely sweet,
love's child, entwined with death's heartbeat,
a love making of shadows, a fragile embrace,
where vulnerability finds its place.

Intertwined Realities

Bask not in the predictable warmth from above,

But observe a realm where no constraints exist.

A cascade of instants unveiled, seen anew,

Each breeze, a narrative cryptically spun.

Perceive the spectrum, the highs and the lows,

As elegance cavorts under skies unsettled.

In quietness, comfort and tranquility bloom,

By the marvels of the untamed, compelled.

Yet within the wonder, an opaque dread casts,

A memory of life's contrasts, yet unfulfilled.

For smiles might mask the unshed tears,

And beneath mirth, melancholy could be stilled.

Nevertheless, within the abyss of wretchedness,

A faint luminosity insists on persisting.

A maze of sentiments, complex and raw,

Emblems of our spirit's undying resisting.

Behold the endeavors, the tribulations, the zeal,

As beings entangle both brightness and obscurity.

Within life's mosaic, you carve your segment,

Observing the narrative of relentless tenacity.

Welcome not the daylight's brush upon the horizon,
Nor let the zephyrs transport your exhalations.
Within these instances, shrouded and radiant,
Lies your quest, your beacon's foundations.

By these observations of existence, you rise unshaken,
Welcoming every fluctuation, the sublime and severe.
For it's within these shifts of the scale,
That life's raw quintessence draws near.

In the Stillness of the Town

No rooster's chant breaks the mute dawn,

The slumber of streets, uninterrupted, drawn.

Cock-a-doodle-doo!

Or could there be roosters, stilled by dreams,

Hidden away in corners, it seems?

Daybreak's touch fails to grace

The somber procession of days' embrace.

Cock-a-doodle-doo!

Whose departure went unnoticed,

As silent as those who've long since floated,

Their names erased by time's indifferent hand

Above the scaffold's grim, lonely stand.

What essence remains?

In the still waters left by time's refrains,

Only shadow-dwellers sing beneath night's cloak.

A rooster's call might rise,

Yet finds no echo in hollowed chests—

No soul to wake, to spark

A solitary flame, igniting the dark

Upon the city's ancient walls.

Or is it solitude itself that rests, void of hope,

Harboring only dreams that elude and cope,

Fleeting, leaving naught but whispers near?

Cock-a-doodle-doo,

A sound, formless to sleepers here,

A misplaced anthem lost in the void.

Who has vanished into silence deep,

Who endures within the pause, awake, yet asleep?

Cock-a-doode-doo!

From "In Exile"

December 18, 2016

Infinite Longing

Where alleyways concede to the waves' soft call,
The albatross stretches its pinions, standing tall,
A testament to your essence, my love.
Through mists' embrace along this secluded way,
Abodes resonate with a natural sigh each day,
Their narrow frames bid open—ablaze with life,
For your remembrance, my love, amid strife.

And the zephyr,
It nestles in stillness across the wide expanse;
Each pause a canvas for the ocean to undress its truth,
In love with you, my love.

At the edge where water meets the sky's endless gaze,
A child sits nude on the wind's lap, grows old in haze,
In the ache of anticipation for you.
While birds, weighed by song, depart,
Resigning their dreams to nests unfound, unmade,
Vanishing beyond the yawn of time's cascade.

From "Echos of Ardor"
April 1988, Toronto

In Sorrow

Awaiting the enameled chain of your smile,

I awaken old longings,

Ancient wounds,

Despair and bygone dreams.

Everything conspires to a heart-wrenching lament,

Enticing us,

Dragging our ashen souls

Into their silence.

Antiquity, decay,

The deep grooves of a dagger on the heart,

And all that should be buried

Guides us back to painful returns—

To desire, to rise,

Within the realm of past inheritances.

And to pass—

Another departure,

In the churn of familiar humiliations, unknown to you.

From the collection "Melodies of Ecstasy"

August 1988, Toronto

In the Pursuit of Liberation

Though I see my lips stitched together now

And witness my agile feet

In chains and shackles,

I have come to grasp the value of bright days.

Yet, I can steal no lover's heart,

Nor become infatuated with the temptations of new love.

Even though

I am steeped in grief for those weightless birds

That soared at will,

Abandoned me in their flight,

I feel that

My heart captures the pursuit of liberation.

Invocation

In the canopy of skies,

extend your hand gently, caress the scarred skin you've known,

draped over my bones, pulled tight across my spirit.

Reach out—before I am left

a charred black hole in the void,

nameless, orbiting a weary exile that becomes eternal—a minuscule singularity

sustaining light from lost meteors.

Invoke the Deity of fondness,

extend your hand, and let warmth guide the dark.

From the collection "Chants of Mysticism"

October 1988 – Toronto

In the Crucible of My Heart

Ignite it, right here

within my heart's chamber,

for it has been scorched to such an extent

that it does not fear your untimely discharge.

Here,

a restless fish longs,

yearning for the sea's vast embrace,

where waves murmur secrets of desire.

From the collection "In the Hope of Flight"

December 1985, Ahwaz

Journey of Love

Begin the journey
of love
with an open heart
and a curious mind.

Follow the path
of whispered secrets
and treasure,
uncovering the mysteries
that dwell within.

Embrace the unknown,
for it holds the key
to infinite possibilities.

Let your spirit soar,
free of doubt,
and find solace
in nature's beauty,
where even our shadows
dance with the dark.

And when you reach
the end of this journey,
may you discover

that love was not
the destination,
but the very essence
woven into the path itself.

Lament for a Tiny Tomb

Alone, in my lone chamber, tears descend,

Silent, within the stillness of my cell,

A grief profound for the soul that did rend,

The radiance from your lips, where love did dwell.

For one who traded freedom of the heart,

For fleeting joys, in moments passing by,

I weep for them, who feared love's fragile art,

And doubted their capacity to comply.

Devoid of you, my tears cascade and flow,

In solitude, where sorrows fiercely roam,

Above a dampened patch of earth, I grieve,

It stifles me, this tiny, sacred tomb.

Within my heart, a lament softly cries,

For love's demise, where only darkness dwells.

Lantern

Amidst serene waters,

A leaf pirouettes gracefully on the pond's stillness,

Its reflection shimmering like a fleeting memory.

No zephyr stirs in this stillness,

No leaves pirouette and descend

In the cyclic dance of this leaf,

Spinning within its own embrace

In the marsh's tranquil hold.

No echoes reverberate,

No melodious breath,

As if time itself

Tires of the clock's hands' motion,

Heavy with their load,

In futile reflection of their vain, fruitless nature.

***

Above the expanse of water,

On a peaceful, slumbering bridge,

Woven of silence, it divides

Me from my beloved,

Balancing on solitude's rail,

I contemplate the play of memories,

Each one a whisper in the wind.

And within, in the delicate flight of dandelions,

Ensnared within the cruel clasp of thorns.

I glimpse a figure far away,

Beyond time's grasp,

Calling my name,

Her voice melding with sparrows' chirps and the moon's luminance,

Fading into the chorus of crickets,

Breaking the silence.

Approaching footsteps I hear,

Borne on a breeze from distant recollections,

Swiftly passing, like shadows fading in dusk.

I survey my surroundings,

None in sight,

Save unripe grape clusters,

Blossoming on out-of-reach boughs,

Yearning for more time,

And the weathered hollows of wooden casks,

Parched while awaiting the grapes.

***

Old lanterns flanking the bridge,

Though empty-handed,

Though beyond reach,

Cast light upon the path,

Illuminating the shadows of what once was.

From the collection "In Exile"

April 10th, 2016

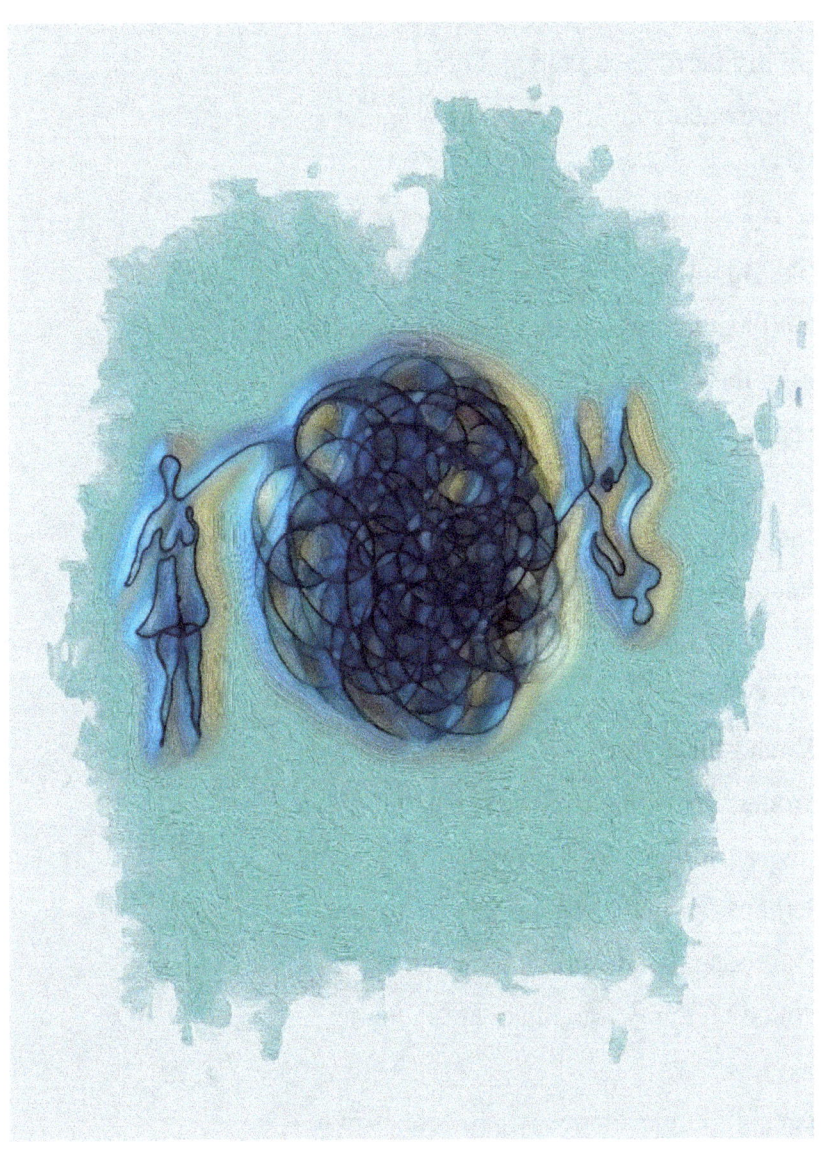

Leather Threads

I bound them,

Tightly laced each vein and bone,

Where once your love had softly shone.

I fastened them,

Like lightning striking in the dark of night,

With leather threads that damply protest and jeer,

So in the searing yearning of day,

Aching for you in every way,

Craving your embrace, I'd gently sway.

They grip and tear me apart,

Fracture my bones, a lingering ache in my heart.

I tied them,

Wound them near,

Around my veins, enclosing what I hold dear.

For you were never truly mine,

Perhaps our paths will never intertwine,

Your once radiant smile, a distant sign,

Unknown to my longing heart's incline.

Yet still, in the silence where echoes play,

I trace the shadows of love's lost array.

Let me

I plead not to divine ears, but to your tender grasp I reach,

Seeking solace, not eternal, just a transient reprieve.

Allow me a harbor in your arms, not to ignite desire's flame,

But to breathe in life's pure nectar, to elevate my weary game,

To escape this corporeal prison filled with fading mortal names.

I implore, not the heavens, but your encompassing fold,

A fleeting sanctuary where warmth whispers, yet is bold.

That this eager heart, emblazoned within its cage,

Might sip tranquility through our shared tears—that silent stage,

While outside, the world spins wild, a tempest unconfined,

And in your arms, I seek the calm that chaos left behind.

Let Them Fall

Beneath a zenith's blaze, an unforgiving eye,

Where thoroughfares narrow, dwellings sigh a stifled cry,

A parched hush settles, expectant at the threshold's parting,

Yet aloft, a somber nimbus, its odyssey now charting.

O bearer of tempests, laden with the weep of heaven,

Murmur your ancient lore as you bleed and leaven,

Dispatch your pearls in cadenced descent,

To script a saga on skies, so desolate and rent,

As I cry along your weeping grace, alone,

A stream of solace flows in my heart's quiet tone.

Letter in a Bottle

Oh ocean, keeper of tales so vast,
Your waves whisper secrets of the past.
Upon your shores, my hopes find their floor,
Carry them afar, to the distant moor.

Beneath your gaze, hidden depths abide,
Tears in your eyes, the pain you can't hide.
Soothe my spirit, ocean; serenade my soul
With rhythmic waves that make me whole.

To you, the sea, my letter I confide—
For my beloved; may you soften its stride.
May she feel my warmth in your gentle hold,
In your endless span, let my love unfold.

Speak in ripples, speak in rolling tides,
Moon and sea, in you, mystery resides.
Show the night's allure beneath your sway;
Onward, let my longing in your waves convey.

Vast ocean, gentle, majestic, and grand,
Bear my heart tenderly towards the land,
Where corals sway and their colors ignite—
There deliver my love, both day and night.

Over boundless blue, we'll join as one;

Your waves, the chariot for emotions to run.

With gratitude, I cast this letter, my plea:

Oh ocean, weave our hearts in harmony.

Lightning

What's perceived rarely mirrors truth's domain,
Illusions fleeting, reality's thin pane.
The revered idols, prayers recited through the night,
Fractured branches, birds in hurried flight.
Paths trodden lead to a friend's embrace,
Shrouded in chaos, veils of mystic haze.

Emotions churn, echoes of a dismal lore,
A pursuit, akin to death's relentless roar.
Desires embraced fall short of liberty's plea,
Longings unmet, yearnings wild and free.

A gaze, pure and solemn, weeps a tear,
In solitude, akin to Mary, void of fear.
Smiles bright, gracing lips with tender zest,
Moments cherished, friendships at their best.

But deep within, a lightning bolt ignites,
Trust crumbles to ashes, vanishing from sight.

What's seen but a façade, a shifting screen,
Dreams and desires lost in murky sheen.
No final decree, just estrangement's gloom,
Drifting souls, entwined in shadows' fume.

From the depths, it emerges, consuming the core,

To sepulcher's confines, a cycle to explore.

Leaving in its wake, earth's barren skin,

A void remains, where love had once been.

Limbo

What can I say?
What do I yearn for?
My soul is ablaze,
Like a crucified dove,
Yearning for its release.

I refuse to be seen in sorrow.

Broken, unbidden,
From the dust of birth,
Only if—oh, if only,
If granted the chance, I'd plunge
Into the rugged earth of my homeland,
Merging with its acrid currents,
The embers of my yearnings.
And beneath the deep roots of a grand oak,
Or among tart berries,
New life would burgeon within me.

I refuse to appear bowed in defeat.

What can I express?
What do I long for?
Trapped in limbo, that is where I stand,
With my soul engulfed in flames.

March 1988 - Toronto

From the collection "In Exile"

Lost

Sometimes I ponder deeply, my fears ubiquitous,

How the cosmos itself can seem so dubious.

My own hands and heart incite a subtle terror,

The simple fall of a petal, the repetition of time—

A burden I carry in the quiet confines of my mind.

There are moments when fear engulfs me wholly,

Both in solitude and in the nakedness of timeless instants,

Where no creation stirs, yet fear persists.

If only your tender gaze, laden with a hundred clusters of jasmine,

Could accompany me,

And the symphony of your voice, like rain upon arid plains,

Could echo in the desert of my heart,

Carrying me to wild marjoram flourishing unreservedly.

Where are you, beloved?

Your presence is but a ghostly wisp—

A child lost amidst the boisterous marketplace of endless recklessness,

Tearful and unseen,

As a mother's comforting grasp fades from view.

And my heart pounds with such ferocity

That even the heavens' thunderous roar eludes my ears.

Drenched, shivering, hunched in the boundless town square,

Where nothing but relentless rain falls,

No path's beginning, no morrow's end,

No beacon aglow over an unseen abode at a distance,

Nor the contour of a single star etched upon the dense veil of clouds.

Oh, love,

Invite me to the festivities of my dreams,

Guide my hands across the form of unprotected moments.

Lead me through gardens filled with scented blooms,

To gaze upon the astonishing beauty of women.

Take me to the junctures where time's hands don't repeat their cycle,

And time itself is a flowing virtue.

Oh, love, escort me to confront my fears head-on,

Face to face with my childhood's echo

In that vibrant, bustling market—

Before my hands relinquished the softness of yours.

From the collection "In Exil"

September 19, 2016

Lost in Twilight

Lost in this twilight haze, I stand,
Alone, unheard, in this barren land.
I seek the dawn's fiery sign,
A beacon bright in this dark design.

With every wound upon this ground,
My weary eyes search for the sound
Of echoes from a blood-stained past,
Where shadows linger, cold and vast.

I remember the bloodshed of years gone by,
Wolves lurking in silence, ready to pry.
I will raise my voice, shatter this shroud,
Yearning for freedom, breaking the crowd.

In search of a new beginning, I'll depart,
Venturing deep into the ocean's heart.

Love Bird's Song

In fleeting moments, free dove of the sky,

Alight upon my chest, feel love's soft sigh.

Heeding the melody of a bird's refrain, encased,

Nestled within my heart's abode, trembling, scared.

Lovers Embrace The Silence

Words falter, tears cascade, failing love's parade,

Chests rise with sighs, emotions running deep,

From the depths, vague visions stealthily creep.

A steadfast fish, unwavering in its flow,

Through the river's sinuous, determined show.

Bodies guided, with purpose in their claim,

Lovers entwine in silence, their bond aflame,

Like the sun's silent steps, commanding, untamed.

A coffin's grip, firm and unrelenting,

Detains a soul, where love is never relenting.

Beloved, witness the fray in this fragile play,

Heeding the melody of a bird's refrain, encased.

Stay with me, I plead and beseech!

Lest they bury our hearts beneath darkness' breach.

Lament of Agony

Mourning echoes, anguished cries kick dust,

Blood streams weave down faces, a sorrowful flood,

Countless mothers wail for children silenced in slaughter.

While the innocent weep,

For the sweet milk of comfort now dried in deserted veins,

As women await death, bound to the noose's embrace,

Longing for the children they won't hold again.

The nation's people, shackled, lament and howl,

Homeland hung high, and their grief—

A river mighty, eroding stone,

Carves the canyons of men's eyes, brands their brows

With unspeakable terrors,

And on the grace of young maidens,

A wide channel of blood etched deep.

***

Agony they raise,

Their cries rend the heavens,

Plucking hairs from their weeping scalps

At abundant tombs, unnumbered.

Speak not to me,

Desire not of me,

To drown in ethereal love

When a brother, for the 'crime' of love, is led to captivity.

And weary shoulders abandon their burden on towering pillars,

Leaning back,

Drawing smoke,

Retreating into oneself,

While vicious hands of wind play upon the pole,

Claiming a sister's lifeless body as a toy.

***

Ah,

My sister unshrouded!

     The cries I hear.

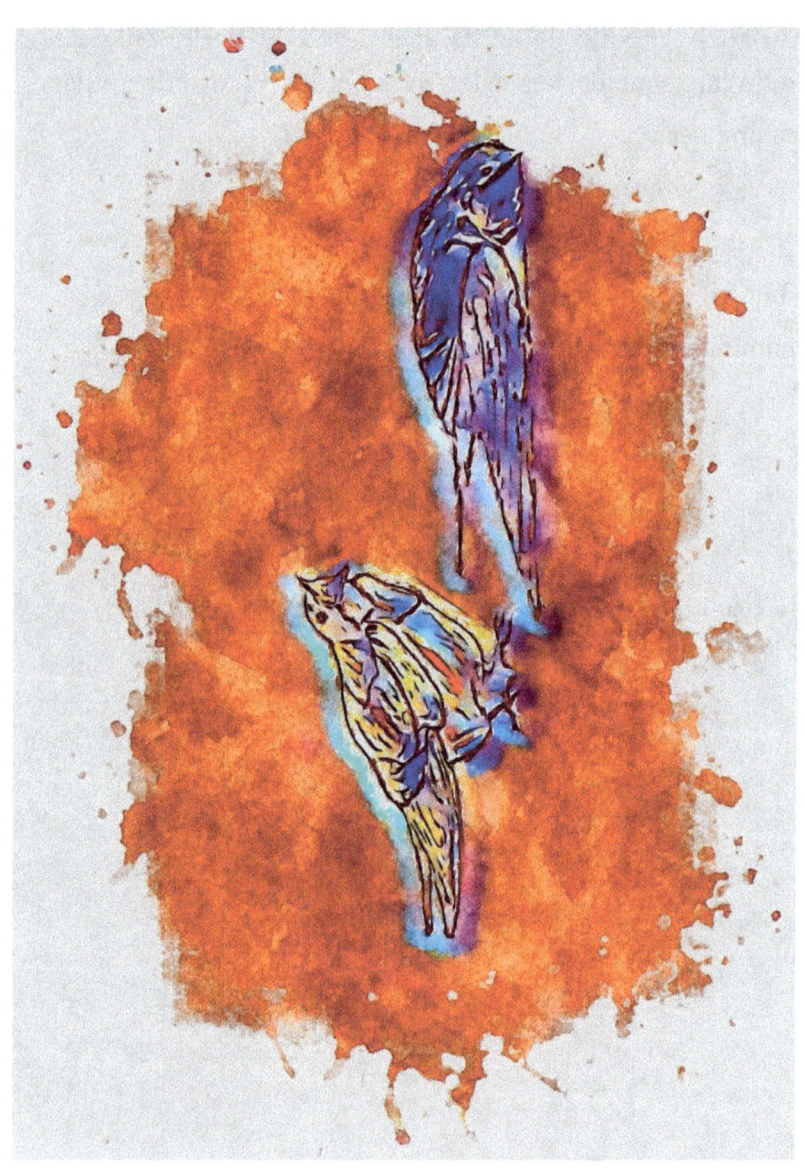

Martyr

Unending azure,
boundless and wide,
yet nestled deep within,
a crimson tide.

A piercing barb,
where anguish resides,
a solitary vessel in love's grasp denied.

Scars etched deep,
in relentless pursuit,
thoughts of celestial orbs,
bloodied dreams, mute.

Blue horizons breached,
like torrents untamed,
boundaries blurred,
in whispered myths unnamed.

Within this twilight's deceptive hue,
a veil of falsehoods,
cloaking the true,
yet beneath the shroud,
resilience breaks through.

My City

With barren trees and tamarisk edges,
innumerable palms,
my beautiful Ahvaz,
scent of blossoming orange blooms
carried through spring morning breezes.

Silence of nights is broken
by the chirping crickets,
swallows
resting on the heavy lids of air, worn and stifling.

Ahvaz,
my unmatched and beautiful city!
With a spring as brief as a smile,
and a summer as long as three furrows of a frown,
beneath an orange sky,
where no trace of stars remains.

Young girls, verdant life, laughter on lips,
a narcissus tucked in hair,
by riverbanks
where the sparkle of lost stars shines
in the depths of their dark eyes from afar.

This is how I arrive at autumn,

with leaves falling in a thousand hues,
and the rain washing away
the night's continual silence
upon the weary earth,
singing pleasant melodies.
A winter fleeting as a shooting star
on the warm bosom of an orange night,
bearing hope for spring
to hearts frozen solid
beneath the night's heater.

Ahvaz, now,
a cursed city,
sullied with dust,
a land scorched by time.
A tale of oil plundered,
re-imposing the dominance of conquests
once again upon Iran.
Ahvaz, my beautiful city,
the home of migratory sparrows,
city of pigeons and skilled fanciers
on green rooftops,
amid the sprouting grass of spring.

Ahvaz, my city,
an unfinished place,
a cry seated in silence,

rebellion thrashing on the river's banks,

thumping within the city's chest.

Ahvaz,

city of dawns where blood

strikes against the chest of the sky,

and the chariot of the sun

sets fire to body and soul,

until evening slumbers in humid air and dust.

Ahvaz,

our oppressed city!

A land of blood, soil, and a raging sun

in the air.

From the collection "In Search of My Land"

January 31, 2018

My Heart

I transformed into a hand,
pouring a bowl of water upon the land,
quenching all that parched and dried,
reviving earth's veins so wide,
and memories lost in the vast soil's expanse.

I poured and was drawn
into dark channels, forever gone.
As solitude immersed me deep,
I felt no spring's joyous leap.

Particles of silt clung to my frame,
to my spirit, and the moisture I shamelessly aimed.
Cracks began to form upon my lips,
my skin reflecting the desert's arid trips.
The once vivid blue in my eyes did fade,
no longer a canvas for your cascading hair's shade.

And my heart,
oh, my heart, that loved the boundless sea so vast,
believed that before all this could pass,
it should have spilled thirstily on life's very last,
and my very soul.

From the collection "Songs of Longing"

April 1989 - Toronto

Mist

Every morning, tyranny of mist;

an arcane drizzle born from the sea,

a hexed tint lunges at me—

an unyielding battalion of vapor,

absent of hue or moniker,

sets its sights on ransacking my fervid heart,

impaling it upon its lancet at dawn.

A mist of breaths, akin to exhalation,

ascends from the smoldering core within—

a mist dipped in the sorrowful indigo of anguish

that, once upon a time, from a celestial motherland,

carried me adrift to unnamed soils.

Ever since, when zephyrs shepherd

my tempest-tossed musings to those ancient lands;

my heart, aching for the solace of dreams,

quivers to life;

I gaze, arrested by sheer wonder, to behold—

the horizon smothered in lamenting mist,

a barrier between me and every instant that withers along with my exhales,

a veil between me and every breath that burgeons in my soul's enclave—

a fog plucking the strings of sorrow and weeping upon my spirit's lyre.

And to this strain, harmonizing with the drowsing haze,

a cadre of sightless minnesingers roams, intoning—

minstrels devoid of wish to witness anew,

minstrels whose chalice brims solely with heart's crimson.

Exhausted by these enclosing nebulous chains, I coax myself:

Arise, shed the fetters of the voyage,

bear no stockpile of answers, nor despondency,

venture upon this forlorn twilight path;

and I whisper to my being,

from here to the edged terminus, where all passageways cease,

no further gambits lie in wait.

For as I embark upon this journey,

it alone will dictate the span to traverse,

stripped of dread for misplacement or desertion in the cloaking eve.

But each attempt at standing,

with pilgrim's staff in grip

and hope nestled in breast,

reveals to me—

the path, swathed in dense fog, erases itself from view;

the road has rescinded from remembrance,

or perhaps within the path's recollection, I am effaced—

perhaps the road itself,

and in the labyrinthine surge that uprooted my existence—

the deluge that snatched me from my native soil,

hurling me upon this land afar,

has effaced itself in its own tumult,

becoming invisible, lost to the depths.

Each night, until death's solemn seal is affixed,

I dream of a luminous path ahead,

an avenue untouched by mist,

where no vaporous thief lurks

to veil a single recollection from my grasp,

where memory refuses to play the charlatan,

concealing itself behind a blind curtain of haze.

from "In Exile"

March 28, 2016

Mojgan

Years long,
neglectful wind,
eavesdropping clouds,
playmates of the moon,
on the horizon, boundless blue.

The cocoon splits the chest
in a dream of two wings,
yearning for flight beyond the grove.

Asleep in a narrow grove,
her share, a delicate blueness,
a trace of blood, the yellow animosity ahead,
and a bird in flight,
a fleeting shadow of desire.

She turned and sewed her eyes onto passing,
no one was coming after her,
and no one was calling her name.
A child of the wind, she remained,
with no hand of affection laid upon her.

Oh,
the long eyelashes of wind,
sweep the dust away.

With one eye in the sky and another on the earth,

look after her green skin, beloved,

born from that very anticipation,

high-winged and broad-shouldered,

her smile like a mountain lily,

her blood, drop by drop,

a blend of sun and autumn's dance—

keep her safe with gentle care.

From the collection "SFrenzied Songs"

August 1987 - Karachi

Moments in Time

A gentle breeze of spring stirs,

as the spring clouds shed their tears,

emerald green shoots arise.

The song of love, echoing from rooftops,

once again, it arrives—

the bird of love, freed from its cage, soars high into the sky.

Upon my hushed lips,

your laughter, so exquisite,

nurtures a tender bud.

A soft breeze whispers through the air,

love's turbulence weaves a new design,

savoring the essence from every soulful cup.

The spirited horse of desire

gallops from dusk till dawn,

the ears of my heart resonate with your voice.

Yearning for your presence paints the tapestry of my heart with joy,

unveiling another bittersweet ache,

igniting a blaze of anticipation and sparks.

A gentle breeze of spring embraces,

the branch of love entwines, like morning glories in fervor.

The restless lover, hopeful for union,

discards attire at the threshold,

a cry wells up in the depths of his heart—

once again, it gallops,

the fragrance of countless memories tiptoes into the recesses of my heart.

As laughter traverses the path, reaching the threshold,

sorrow arrives fleetingly, then departs,

leaving echoes of moments intertwined.

From the collection "Songs of Exile"

28th February 2017.

Moonlit Verse

I rest, beholding the moon's tender luminescence,
a mirror of obsidian, reflecting the heavens' quiet dance.
I rest, ensnared by lunar whispers, mild,
adrift in splintered echoes, time's child.

To her, the night's silent sovereign, I yearn,
sunk deep in sagas unspoken, I turn.
Oh, moon, keeper of whispers, of nocturnal hopes,
bathe the dusk in your silver, carving new slopes.

Steer me through the shadows with your steadfast poise,
a gentle sentinel in life's relentless noise.
Beneath your muted radiance, enigmas gently shift,
breathing stories of ardor in a silent drift.

I sit, confronting the moon in quiet reverence,
swathed in its splendor, touched by its permanence,
where the secrets of the wind reside,
echoing the dreams that in stillness abide.

Mother

You, who packed and departed forever,
with no tears and no hint of envy,
not even a fleeting sigh.
In your leaving, you took nothing but my heart.

I remember autumn's arrival,
leaves of orange and yellow wailing,
a crow perched on a branch,
waiting to snatch my eyes.

Along a dimly lit alley,
a whispering wind brushed my ear,
rattling doorknobs.
I beheld with my own eyes
my heart gone with you,
leaving me behind—
no tears remaining to rise
from the lonely bed,
overflowing the footprints of your steps
with a stream of melancholic blue.

When you left, I vividly recall
yearning to rise,
to shut the door on the world,
struggling to pull the doorknob.

I dammed a river

flowing between my home and the neighbors,

upon my father's grave,

buried in this garden.

I set free two canaries

from their cage,

into the open sky,

a tribute to the love within your heart.

And I sat upon the earth,

gazing into the eyes of that crow,

which had no rush to steal my sight.

From the collection "In Exile"

November 16, 2016

Night's Whispers

She strikes the horizon's fiery edge,

igniting the night's awe with her touch.

Her gentle hand delivers darkness to the day,

guiding me through the veiled path

where the secrets of the wind reside.

The wind, like a lover's caress,

whispers across my longing heart.

In its embrace, my desires bear scars,

yet I yearn for the solace it brings.

Yet the night, my eternal companion,

will be my refuge, my sanctuary,

only if she, my guiding light, stands beside me.

With her, I traverse the shadows deep,

together confronting the wind's fierce might.

In her presence, I rise like the moon,

embarking on a journey to the ocean's embrace,

where waves cradle dreams and fears in their pulse.

From the collection "Echoes of Sorrow"
June 1988, Toronto

Nightingales

You once whispered:
"Spring will arrive, flowers will bloom, hyacinths will emerge."
Yet now, gaze upon our fate,
as autumn fades and winter twirls in,
the earth, stripped of scents,
remains cloaked in silence and uncertainty.

You spoke of the earth humming
with the fragrance of blossoms.
But here, shadows linger,
where in the quiet of night a solitary bloom
rests upon a stone—perhaps a memory or farewell.

You reassured:
"The sorrows of friends will dissolve; smile!"
Yet one by one, from this fleeting time, our companions
have slipped away, leaving our home
adrift in a haze of unspoken grief.

Why did you say:
"In the desert, the nightingale will sing"?
You were our song in this wilderness.
Why did you depart this realm?
Why now?
Why without us?

In dreams, perhaps,

the nightingales tread softly, or do they?

Nightmare Terror

In the heart of night, I arose,
On a bed of my own solitude,
From the grip of a breathtaking dream
That seemed to pull me close.

My skin turned cold, standing on end,
My breath retreats, my voice is lost,
Deep within the arid inferno,
This fear, in my mother's womb, began its cost.

Sometimes, I whisper to myself,
Life's but a brief span between dreams.
In pursuit of hollow desires, I surrendered—
To a fleeting spark, my essence lost, it seems.

A colorful patch, a crooked stitch,
On the torn fabric of my soul's scheme.

From this relentless terror, perhaps my last,
My body quivers and shakes.
Between lucid moments and the vast sleep,
The soulmate waits by my door, her heart aches.

But as I rise to open for her,
I see, in horrifying states,

Someone, my twin, but slightly pallid,
Hair disheveled, with predatory traits.

More ravenous than a pack of wolves,
Residing within my shape.
He pushes me to answer the door,
My tongue heavy, my escape thwarted more.

One hand reaching for the door to ensure
My soulmate is safe once more,
The other, seeking a way to stop
This bloodthirsty doppelgänger at bay.

Fear of the imminent clash,
Love that's a mere step away,
Death that dwells within,
And a scream stuck midway...

What can I convey?
Every night, from my lonely bed, I spring,
Ensuring the door remains closed, letting no one in,
In this dance of shadows, where nightmares begin.

Nude

No one has ever desired my soul so nude—

Not my mother,

Not my lover,

Not even the reflection staring back,

And not even myself.

O Azur Cloud

Atop a ladder reaching into the clouds,

I pause for a breath to carry on,

contemplating deep valleys below

and towering mountains cradling the sky.

I gaze upon my bent stature

and the lofty dreams I've shouldered.

O azur cloud,

sweep me along with you,

and drizzle my essence,

drop by drop,

upon my thirsty homeland—

and a path that's clear,

where my spirit would roar free.

Ocean Souls

My body!
Oh, vessel of mine,
Shall grace the banquet of fish,
While my weary bones seek solace
In the depths of the ocean's embrace.

No trace of my pulsing veins
Shall taint the flavor of the sea,
Nor reveal the fiery secret I bear.

Oh, gentle waves,
Sincere waves that crash,
Will you caress the resting place of my kin,
And softly kiss my mother's feet
In our final reunion,
So she may recognize me once more in your embrace
And hold me close again?

In the corners of my vision,
Fish lay their precious eggs,
And one day, my skull's remnants
Shall sense the journey
Of fortunate souls, with hearts of the ocean,
Who too understand the ache of distance and longing.

Ode to Shabnam

Swept with intensity surpassing tempest gales,

I've plunged into the spirit of the infinite deep.

Tell me, companions, have you witnessed

How the zephyr impregnates the tides with life?

My dear Shabnam,

Even before your genesis,

And before your tears enrich

The ocean's brimming coffers,

Amid the cloud's grieving drift,

I've felt your presence,

Resplendent beyond fall's splendor.

Gifted with your mother's eyes,

Almond-shaped, imbued with the lingering aroma

Similar to that found in sun-kissed coffee beans

And in the bloom of almond groves.

Your captivating smile will mirror hers,

Unveiling with the audacity of crimson blooms upon a branch,

And more rebellious than the breaking of waves

On the hardened coral rocks.

Ah, my Shabnam, I am but a descendant of the wind,

To you, I bequeath the cascading autumnal foliage,

Entwined with the somber tunes I play,
In perpetual quest for vernal rebirth.

From "Songs of Intoxication"
May 1988 - Toronto

On Rooftops

On rooftops, they dance naked,
Bloodstained from the blows of the wind,
And hidden among the roots deep down,
Are the young dancing girls.

Let nothing be lost to the wind, my love.
Where is your green home?
Sleeping, burned and colorless in your cocoon,
You've shut the windows tight, not to see me pass,
Fading with the ash color of evenings
And the edges of boundaries.

You've picked a pomegranate to bite,
In which blood resides—
Blood of crucified pride and bitter years,
Sharp as the sting of a dagger,
So acquainted with water.

My love,
Where is our home in the autumn's onslaught,
With a brutal rider on horseback
And a bloody dagger in hand,
Amidst whirlwinds of memories?

I desire a home as vast as the sea,

And sleep,

A crystal orb with the moon,

Above bright meadows of the cosmos.

In the twists of the dark forest,

Or on waves tainted with soil,

With a home upon my shoulders,

And a clear pathway.

Only with You

No!

I won't, I shan't come,

I won't see, I won't weep.

Though I know your secret scars run deep,

I refuse to glimpse that inverted shape,

Sculpted in solitude from me.

Even if I sense the silent screams of your wrath,

Restless in your stillness,

The fears that torment me, I hold back,

Refusing to speak.

Your trembling shoulders

No longer find peace with me,

And my heart, oh, my heart,

On your bare shoulder finds no rest, no glee.

No, I won't come back, won't return in cries,

My frame shattered, shoulders shaking,

I deny.

Such profound love that mocked Farhad's axe,

Making light of its strike on the heart of stone,

And saw Majnun's wild escapades

As mere child's innocent drone.

This love so deep, it summoned the strength
Of a thousand men's might,
Making the shimmering star cluster
Naked in my eyes, so bright.

This profound love, my inception,
Began my release, my exception,
Rescuing my soul from nightmares' toll,
Like a disturbed pond, or a swift stream's turn.

No, I won't let go, won't play the tune,
For my end with you just begins so soon.
The start, once within your reach,
Now leached from memory, out of touch.

Oh, if only I could take you,
Like a sharp arrow in a bow's grip,
Aimed at the heart, ready for the trip,
Into my heart's deep lakes, to you,
To witness the stillness approaching the end,
To see these lakes, without you, can't mend.

To witness, with open eyes,
The vision of a fountain, across galaxies it lies,
Begins with you, travels with you,
Leading us to suns of love anew.

O Serendipitous Spirit

Tranquility eludes the epochs,
Peace remains a distant lover.
A moment mourns, a widow's hair cascades,
Yet sorrow's thirst is never quenched.

In this realm where chaos reigns,
Restless seeds scattered, seeking purpose.

Blessed is the spirit,
Dwelling in death's fleeting minutes,
Not estranged from life's transient instances,
Nor wearied by its delights.
For within the facade of existence,
They sought emancipation,
Always yearning for tenderness
In all that could soften their essence.

O serendipitous spirit,
That embraced the world
In its most fragile moments,
Fearless in the face of mortality,
Nurturing exquisite aspirations
Within a vibrant heart.

From the anthology "In Pursuit of Flight"

March 1986 - Ahvaz

Our Love

Within my heart's core, a gilded light does burn,
A secret flame, ignited by your glance,
A chorus of hushed tones, tender and divine,
Our spirits merge, entwined in a seamless dance.

We sway through twilight, in syncopated grace,
In unison, we let go, our spirits embrace.
As if a loom threads its careful art through air,
Our love unfolds, a rare and precious masterpiece.

Parting

Alas, heart, departing shattered,

With eyes now drowned in sanguine tears,

And aspirations steeped in despair,

A whirlwind of present memories and past,

Dust and turbulence covering all,

Over hearts and buried remnants entombed.

What awaits she in her vigil,

In a night claimed by sorrow?

Where mist chants its somber elegy,

And tears begin their slow descent,

Upon her beloved's remembrance—

A crystal of agony and crimson bloom—

Silent pathways stretch wide,

Leading into the void.

Voiceless, without guitar or melody on her lips,

By that small, secluded window,

With long chains of her tresses

Reaching toward the moon's embrace,

Each strand's a weep for what we have lost,

Echoing through the silent night.

From "Ecstatic Songs" collection,

September 1987

Prisoner

In twilight's gentle melody, where all retire,
Her trembling body, touched by the cold and arid,
She crossed the threshold,
Fear and haunting, terror shimmering in her eyes.
She whispered, "I have eluded the cruel dungeon's torment,
And sprinted down every path in a single breath,
To surrender my life in your embrace."

Silently, she arrived,
Her heart immersed in the anguish of crimson,
Traversing the winding path of garden memories,
Where fragrant blooms weep in the dusk.

"Oh God, arise and draw near,
Enfold me in your arms before I depart.
I have firmly clasped the hands of the indomitable woman,
Time and time again,
To bestow the warmth of hope,
As a gift to the earth and to you.
Oh God, arise and draw near."

***

The wind stood motionless, frigid and still,
And the lands lay fragmented like shards of ice.

Her blood cascaded upon the earth,

Yet still she sang, rich and melancholic,

With my heart harmonizing,

"Oh earth, oh companion,

Ignite the flame of tomorrow."

From the collection "In the Yearning for Flight"

Tehran, 1363 (1984)

Purgatory

What words can capture
This eternal wait?
When my soul, suspended,
Like a dove in flight, held by an unseen fate.

I yearn to hide my fragile state from view.

Severed, not by choice, from my birth's embrace,
Oh, how I ache,
How fervently I ache,
To merge with my homeland's bitter taste,
Where aspirations crumble to ashes, bitter and grim.
Let verdant roots of pine or wild berry intertwine,
A dance of contradiction, nature's serpentine.

I shun the sight; on bended knee, I plea,
For solace in this solitude, a gentle hand to see.

What sentiments can I convey,
What longings reside,
When I am caught in purgatory's sway,
Where my essence burns, a tempest inside.

Purity

I stand here,
in this very place,
in my empty body,
under a flowing stream,
to cleanse my existence,
my gaze,
my thoughts,
my soul, and my essence.

I stand here,
imprisoned within this form,
with the searing breaths of negation,
transforming heavy raindrops into warm, dense mist,
gradually, tenderly enveloping me—
laden with abundance,
the blood of life,
and hues of madness,
where the self shatters.

Here, I tread upon a drenched path,
more saturated than the relentless rush of water,
scorched by the furnace of the heart.
No fear resides within my chest,
no melody graces my lips,
not even

the yearning for another's presence.

I stand here, in this very place,
not elsewhere,
soaked to the core,
contemplating that final breath,
at the rusted loop of life's door—
the last breath, with no breath to follow,
leaving no trace of my being.
In that narrow moment,
I dissolve into water,
like a rock made of limestone and sigh.

I dissolve, I comprehend,
and my body
diminishes in the furnace of negation,
like the waning moon.
Although I know
that neither my body is pure, nor my gaze,
nor even my heart—
nonetheless!

from the collection "In Exile",
31st March 6.

Reflections

Sometimes I ponder,

What lacks in me compared to a tree?

Proud limbs reaching toward the boundless clear,

Roots driven deep with might into the firm earth,

Where, not so long ago, the wind sowed its seeds.

Sometimes I wonder,

What lacks in me compared to a thorny bush?

That, in death, tumbles free and unrestrained,

Scattering its essence across the land it flourished.

Or what do I lack

Compared to a bird, singing with a thousand others,

Their chorus ringing from the branches above?

What do I lack, my God,

Compared to a glowworm that, with gentle light,

Illuminates existence like a candle on a dark night?

What do I lack? I do not know,

Only that this lacking leaves my heart bleeding.

The air of my land weighs heavy on my soul,

A land where melodious birds have sung to the essence of my being.

Each time I've fallen to its soil,

Like a young phoenix from ashes, I rise,

Opening my eyes to the dawn of another morning.

Speak not of what I do not know; for years my homeland
Has been a prisoner to the bitterness of chains, daggers, and constraints—
The source of my heart's sorrow; speak not of it.
Do not say that over tumbling thorny thickets,
The blaze is ready with overflowing fire,
That the trees are without birds,
No longer a sanctuary for melodious song,
For they burn in the flames...

What you speak is true,
Yet it is for my homeland
That my heart yearns deeply.

From the collection "In Search of My Land"
October 24, 2017

Remorse

Oh, how the snow silently descends, Chilling the warm, flowing river of blood, Blanketing the earth's bosom with regret.

The earth, lamenting,

Enfolding countless fallen within its embrace. And the moon melts in sigh and mist above

Those who weave the tapestry of history, With fingertips cracked and scarred

With strands of tender, waning moonlight mesh, And delicate strands of moonlight,

In the end, they stitch the blood To the very edge of the clouds.

Oh, the blood absorbed by the earth, And the man who wept before his time,

Alas, the honor now tarnished and mourned.

Rebuke

For poetry, I sought life's breath,
Poetry, conceived for you, and you—
Soul of existence, beyond replace.
Longing to reflect your splendor,
To sculpt your essence, pure, ineffable.

Your allure,
As starlit skies soften
Desert's harsh whisper against my spirit.

Forgiving overseer of my flaws, my missteps
And my verses,
Each a mischievous wisp ascending
On the winds of whimsy.

In wrath's heat,
Your gaze withdrew—
My lush, cherished one!

You, extractor of my heart,
Withholding your luminous shard
To guide my path.
Now, your gaze shuttered from me,
I inscribe, yet unseen by you,
I craft, yet unheard,

I lament, yet unacknowledged,

For

You were the muse from which poetry flowed,

And for you, life itself was pursued.

Pardoner of my failings,

My verses—

From "Lost in the Wind"

June 1999 - Toronto

Resurrection

Through the weight of countless years,
And all the pain and suffering endured,
I find myself in a slumber, devoid of waking,
Longing for a soul to come
To lift this decaying body from the waters' grasp,
A savior to bury my moss-covered bones
In an unnamed corner, deep within my homeland,
To rest eternally in the embrace of the soil.

After all these years,
I yearn for the arrival
Of a presence whose smile's sweetness
Mirrored the warmth of yours,
And whose gentle hands, in ceaseless caress,
Would grant this long-dead flesh
A second chance to rise and thrive.

If only a soul could come,
To carry the weight of these countless years...

From "Lost in the Wind"
April 1998

Reflection's Quest

Tell me, mirror of my core, what do you seek?

In lands once lush, now voiceless and bleak,

Where birds of height in descent are cast,

As vaporous pasts, wraith-like and vast.

What aim bears weight on your scale?

In hushed arenas where silent pleas sail,

Echoes foregone, in the vastness they die;

Spirits yearn and bleed for the sky.

Through divergent roads, donning every guise,

With each notion that hope baptizes,

Stride on, my spirit, take the leap of faith;

Your step may waken the avian wraiths.

Cross my heavens, marred and askew;

In your caress, restoration may ensue.

Requiem of Quietude

Enshrouded in a void, devoid of other souls' reply,

Oh, woe!

The avian has departed its cradle of twigs,

Solitary zephyrs murmur 'cross forlorn boulevards.

In fall—a season once cradling dear remembrances—

Unwove its tapestry with ease, into oblivion dispatched.

And now, in the wake,

A shroud of frost accumulates ahead,

An expanse of sea, fragmented relics of former joys,

There stands a buoyant youth, with life's vigor coursing within;

Aside from these, naught else to appraise.

Oh, woe!

The shore bound sea fowl

Is burdened by pinions too frail to ascend.

Rubi

Ya'Qut!

A beauty robed in garnet from head to toe,

Dame of the twilight glow,

A waiting sentinel in daily vigil

At the four-sided parapet of the watchtower.

Ya'Qut!

A graceful figure of untold agonies,

Keeper of a thousand stifled flames,

With the night's majesty,

In a spiritless abode,

Where silence weighs heavy,

Shattered by tears the ceiling would shed,

Sending shivers of cold dampness through her skin.

Ya'Qut!

A beauty of fierce blazes,

Unburdened by earthly possessions clutched in her grasp,

With a satchel of red

Bearing nothing but a letter of love

And a piece of her beloved's heart, crafted from stone.

Ya'Qut!

Clad in crimson's finest,

A tulip aflame amid the city,

Eternal, from yesterday to today.

Ya'Qut!
Bearing countless streams of crimson in her gaze,
Pouring into the oceanic expanse of her heart—
Fire and tears intermingling,
Fashioning an adornment of her own,
Draped across the chest of nameless lovers galore.

***

Ya'Qut!
Beauty of my sleepless city,
Thousands of captive daughters epitomized by you!
Proud and unresting!
Silent, after all these years,
While a legion of red cup-bearers—
Men and women—
From all corners of this metropolis
Ascend to meet you, standing tall,
At the foot of a tremulous statue of the Sage,
Waving the Kavian banner of love.

Ya'Qut!
Now rest in tranquil peace!
... Tranquil, be at peace.

From the collection "In Search of My Land"

November 7, 7

Scarlet-Chested Bird

What do they seek from me—a soul yearning to soar,
to fall upon the earth
and stain life with mire?
I wish there were someone
to plant a bullet in my heart
before pain drives me mad.

How valiantly I'd stand, a rampart against demise,
gaze fixed upon death,
to free this agitated scarlet-chested bird
ensnared in the thicket of agony.

If only there were someone
who adored me beyond my yearning—
someone to lodge a bullet deep within,
then hang that bloodied sphere
as a necklace against her breast.

Sometimes, in despair, I imagine
leaping from the pinnacle of the tallest edifice,
flying without ever touching ground,
nor dying. Alas, I've realized too late
how fervently in love I am,
and the depths of humanity's bloodlust.

From the poetry collection "In Desire of Flight"

February 2005 - Tehran

Shoulders of Masi

Your shoulders, steadfast, a sanctuary they stand,
Guiding us through rugged terrain and land.
Like tranquil rivers, in secrecy flowing,
They touch the world with a gentle knowing.

Wide and open, your embrace does share,
Where secrets find solace, free from despair.
Tears are welcome; here, hearts find their rest,
A refuge for souls on their journeys' quest.

Oh, unwavering companion, solid and kind,
With humble strength, your spirit aligned.
In the depths of despair, you light the way,
Toward love and hope in a vibrant display.

Nurturer, pillar, and devotion so dear,
"Masi" within, an eternal sphere,
Rekindling friendships with love's soft hue,
Igniting memories, forever renewed.

In passion's embrace, we chart our path,
Amid spirited debates, your guidance vast.
Each night you sow solace in our hearts,
A presence comforting, a treasure that imparts.

Your shoulders, tranquil, a name untold,
Defy time's grasp as our stories unfold.
An artist's hand could never capture
The essence you bear as life's chapters mature.

Dear Masi, do you ever feel the weight
Of whispered secrets at heaven's gate?
Endless joys and lovers' words converge,
In our hearts, an eternal surge.

Neither today nor eternity's clasp
Can claim your essence, an enduring grasp.
This smile, these shoulders, steadfast and true,
A beacon of freedom, forever in view.

To my friend forever, Masi Sari- Rest in Peace

Sense of Shame

If we are the mortals they often speak of,

Divided into factions of "us" and "them,"

I carry the weight of collective shame,

This flawed humanity I embody,

Encased within this flawed frame,

By the wounds of our own being.

Sheidaee 2

Your veins irrigate the fields,
And the crystal essence of your being
Dripping through the earth,
Passing through layers of stone and sorrow,
Past the beds of the departed,
And green roots that cradle memories,
To bare the purity of your heart
In the tiniest crevice of the land.

I feel
Each deep wound
Open a path to the core of your heart,
Where your silence, at the bottom of every abyss,
Dances with the pulse of oceanic tempests.

Clouds find their fertility in you,
And my poetic springs emerge from the tears
Of those clouds—
My words passing through rocks and darkness,
My poetry
Rising from the earth, harmonized
To the beat of your heart.

Siege Upon the Veil of Dawn

The dawn's mist enwraps my haven in a whispering chill,
A shroud tight-clasped where once joy did spill.
Tomb-like silence reigns, a labyrinth of the lost,
Our once jubilant sanctum now by shadows tossed.

Oh, had I known
In your heart—burdened beneath layers of the fog's dense sieve,
Where your steps faltered, unseen, elusive—
I would not have shunned that ghastly specter,
Through that smothering cloak, bearing your hidden despairs,
By your side I'd tread, murmurs of valor in the silence we share...
Had you but whispered
Underneath that canopy obscured, heavy with fate's sway,
That a cruel lance preyed upon your spirit, waiting to flay.

Take heed! For the gleam of reunion wanes,
Yet this fervent ache persists,
For a trail, unveiled,
Guiding to your heart's inner sunbeam, fragile but unswayed.
In this dreamlike grotto, I seek and yearn
For our shared emblem, for joy's sweet encore, once more.

If paths existed, true and clear,
Where beside you I'd stand, spared from fear,

Together embarking, unburdened, soaring to the skies anew,

Sailing towards tomorrow, borne aloft in dawn's renewing hue.

Silence Between Us

In the silence blossomed between us,
Or between me and anyone seeking my heart's sojourn,
I stand amidst a desert,
Not a mere barren expanse, but a salt flat,
Waterless and devoid of verdure,
With no beginning or visible end.

Oh, how unfortunate
In this unfruitful silence,
Where my weary body fissures under its desiccating might—
And my gaze, half-dead,
Slithers from mirage to mirage.
Speak to me, converse with me,
Tell me a story or utter a word.

Here, in solitude,
In soul-scourging quiet that pierces me,
I've strewn seeds sparingly in my throat
With drops of sweet memory,
Nourished by the blood of my heart,
In silence, lest they wither
From the blow of this word or that,
Hoping to break free
From the claws of meaningless moments.

But now, in solitude,

Yearning for a smile from your lips,

A word,

Or a kiss from a distant path, I see

A tree has grown in my crestfallen heart,

As real as a nightmare or the chill of dreamless sleep,

Unyielding to consciousness—

A tree, its branches wrought of silence,

No nest remains upon it, collapsed from fading memory.

Oh, regret, that now, I and this loneliness,

And the tree I once planted

In my abandoned throat,

To find respite from relentless downpour

That cleansed my passageway and led to the open sea—

That I and you might find shelter.

A sanctuary where together we might witness

The power of union, the flight,

Falling to earth, then soaring once more,

In the warm, silent gaze of our eyes.

For God's sake,

Say something to me,

So that your familiar voice,

Hidden in the depths of your heart,

May carve a path to my inflamed soul.

From the collection "Exile"

September 28

Smoke

She left, never to return; my hope has dissolved.

That yearning, now in ashes, my heart still yearns.

I, too, have scorched in the bitterness it held,

Within my chest, a fire that forever churns.

Snow

Snow fell and enveloped us,

piling on the courtyard,

and falling from ceilings such immense amounts

that all but whiteness, and the hue of fog,

vanished from sight.

Ah, the relentless snow of this year,

which, flaunting its sculpted form upon my home's bed,

craves no other lover to gaze upon me.

Beneath a blanket made of snow, I lie,

dreaming of luminous days,

cradling a lover's effigy of frost.

O, snow,

when you melt, take me with your flow

to the clear springs afar,

to my land's deepest thirsts—

where, in your soft embrace,

jasmines and marigolds

peer through windows with longing eyes.

Soil and Solitude

How regal the earth, how it woos the heart within,

And homeland—a word that caresses akin.

Tell me, my comrade,

of my homeland so dear.

Speak to me, my friend,

of resting in that soil, forever near.

Converse with me, finest of fellows, a rarity true,

tell of your enamel-like lofty pride.

A depth so profound that, in exile and grief,

like the sun, it blazes undrowned.

Stand with me, my ally,

in solidarity, bound.

To my dear friend and companion, Nader Niakan

From the collection "Songs of the Soil"

September 3, 1988 - Toronto

Something Lost

Oh, it feels,

an unseen thread has frayed in the space we share,

lodged in our core, it dwells,

tarnishing the twilight's edge,

its wail, sharp, steeped in crimson grief.

Shafts have riven its sinew,

ancient cords have held it fast,

scorched and buried in the earth's warm embrace,

to quell its haunting call,

from the alcoves of our minds,

from the chronicles of all.

Yet, beloved,

those sightless in spirit cannot perceive,

its tendrils entrenched in the bosom of our beginnings,

guarded in the hearts of comrades,

a torrent unyielding, untouched by tainted hands.

A future not so far removed,

it will flourish in bounty,

nourished by the scars of the valiant, upon this terra.

Oh, it feels,

there is a remembrance lost between our exchange,

taking root in us,

such serene essence,

revealing its undying repose,

wandering these shattered realms,

cherished by our innermost.

Therefore, companion,

let's walk upon this hallowed ground,

reaffirm our bonds with unveiled spirits.

Song of the Earth

From the dust, my dead rise
and cry like clouds their endless desires
on the chest of the moon.

I ascended to the heights
and sat alone in solitude.
My heart grew heavy,
contemplating the fine dust,
...and the dust of the dead.

The moon
melted drip by drip,
crying in the dry stream of my veins.

In the depths
beneath silent tombs,
the bodies of the dead—
those who dwell in our yearning for freedom,
for a smile upon our lips,
for the sake of the earth,
and for all,
they beckon the green roots of plants
to call unto themselves.
And a forest,

within my narrow abode, within my heart,

takes root.

Song of Soil

It appears

that a fragment has faded from our recollections.

A part of us, deep within,

that pierced the vastness of the night's core,

splattering it with crimson, like a dagger's thrust.

Oh,

she is executed by a firing squad,

hung by an aged, robust rope.

Then incinerated and laid to rest in an unmarked grave,

perhaps to erase her cries that pierced the night's stillness,

from our memories,

and from the collective consciousness.

These blind-hearted executioners fail to comprehend

that the roots delve deep into the soil,

coursing through the veins of our beloved,

like the unstoppable force of a deluge,

escaping the clutches of unseen oppressors.

They remain oblivious,

unaware

that not too distant,

blooms shall emerge from this blood,

upon the weary heart of the land.

It appears

that a fragment has slipped from your memory and mine,

something entrenched within us.

She, who exudes such serenity,

unearths the hardened chest of his resting place,

and strides upon this ravaged land,

cherished within our hearts.

It is time for us to rise,

resurrect the ancient pledge;

with her heart, stained with blood, let us forge it anew.

From the anthology "Songs of Dust"

September 1987 - Karachi

Silent Wings Unfurled

There is no true joy but what resides in your heart.

Unveil that which you guard;

open the door to the captive bird within, alone, yet sings

inside your chest's caged heart.

Dwell not in sorrow for what has passed;

open your heart—

behold the friend's face,

and lift from your loved one's heart the weight of grief.

Life's splendor isn't just a flower's memory in a garden gone;

life is a single petal

amidst the bloom, where other petals bring

a fragrance that leaves traces

in the memory of a garden.

Do not let your dismayed heart, like a fallen yellow leaf,

be played by autumn's harsh desires.

Our world is a strange dream, a garden full of fruit and thorns—

its highs and lows,

a fleeting chance within this garden's expanse,

brief as a sharp spear path thrown,

swift in passing, till upon the beloved's chest it rests.

Let not sorrow nest inside your heart;

there is no joy

but in the warmth of companion's talk.

Spread your hands wide,

grasp the fruit from branches high;

grant that caged bird within the power to soar.

From branches hungry, it shall pass,

where no taller tree can cast its shadow more.

From the collection, "In Search of My Land"
November 1st, 1980

Silent Curvature

If only I dwelled in the cool of dew-kissed twilight,
within the green bend of a leaf
rolling along a slumbering road,
curving beneath the moon
and escaping to distant horizons.

If only in the arc of an encounter I could live,
with leaves of tumbling memories
stretched to the crescent moon's embrace.

If only I thrived in the curvature of connection,
beneath the refuge of a cloud fragment,
free from sharp edges
that might wound me.

Strangely, I have understood
that with you, all is in curvature—
the path of your gaze tracing my desires,
the humility of each defeat,
or a sin born of neglect and despair.

With you,
how well I grasp the curvature of moments,
the bend of a leaf, the sleeping roads,
though you've never been

kinder to me than the coolness of shade.

From the collection "Songs of Passion"
Summer 1987, Karachi

Spring's Resurgence

Beyond the refuge of my silent mound,
spring whispers across yellowing thicket floors.
Verdant life sweeps the plains and hollows,
a raucous spring heralding vitality's roar.

Yet in this heart of mine, a piteous tale—
pierced and deeply scored by countless blades—
a heart drenched in its own failing blood,
fatigued and entombed within my core.

This heart, it seems, cannot find its release,
bound in the stranglehold of its own lacking peace,
to blossom forth, to mend its rips and frays,
at the threshold of a dear one's warm embrace.

From "In Exile,"
March 23, 2016

Springtime Vibes

Spring's breath whispers anew,
tearful clouds of the season weep.
From tears of joy to self-awareness in rebirth,
fresh green reappears in mystic beauty,
unfurling its delicate hue.

The swallow of love, from every rooftop glimpse of you,
takes flight once more, ascending high, a spiraling leap.
Upon my silent lips, a bud of your laughter sown,
a new blossom takes shape, quietly grown.

Spring's breath whispers anew.
The stir of love weaves through hearts;
rhythms undulate as souls imbibe in mirth.
Desire, a stallion drunk on your presence, starts
its nightly quest for your aura's worth.
My heart's ear, keen, hears your call once again.
Yearning paints my spirit's canvas in joyous stain,
old pains scatter, fervor sparks within to sustain.

Spring's breath whispers anew.
Branches bend with love, clinging vines bow.
The restless lover, torn with hopeful reunion,
sheds his garb for love's fervent vow,
a cry of passion, a wild heart's opinion.

Again he flees, seeking that tender trace,

memories perfuming the heart's embrace.

Spring's breath whispers anew.

Your laughter approaches, a herald at the door.

Sorrow lingers but a moment, then it too will soar

in memory of our beloveds,

transforming grief into a melody once more.

Star of Fate

In the stillness where the wind whispers not,

where voiceless clouds trace the sky forgot,

love persists, tears marking a steep journey's plot:

a solitary steed presses on,

its guiding reins, now foregone.

Oh, to become an astral gleam,

or a cloud's pure, drifting dream.

Freed from this human desert's sting,

transformed to downy flake,

gracing the moon-washed pane for someone's heart to wake,

and understand through silent take:

"Behold,

the fateful star in the cold,

the burdened soul from stories old."

A silent dance, no cloud to crowd,

in the muted embrace of wind's muffled shroud.

The earth bows in tranquil rain,

as if to honor love's refrain.

Stay with Me, My Love

Words weep with their inadequacy to voice love,

my chest heaves with a sigh,

vague images emerge from the depths.

A slippery fish

does not lose its way in the sinewy muscles of the river;

limbs do not tread in vain.

Lovers know the silence,

brimming with connection

like the sun's footsteps, noiselessly trodden.

The sinews of a casket

in earth imprison a heart

that never throbs with anything but love.

Beloved, now the struggle commences—

moss and love's muscles locked in combat.

Oh, stay with me!

Lest they plant the heart in a stony sepulchre,

where echoes of our dreams are forever silenced.

Bijan Pedram

From the collection "Songs of Passion"

August 1988 - Graz

Stay with Me

In your presence,

beneath the earth's embrace,

below the roots where love stands firm,

your kindness blooms!

You have journeyed into the depths with me,

you have entered the shadows alongside me.

I sprouted from the sanctuary of worms,

while you came on the wings of melodious birds,

and our meeting was a hidden haven

for our scorched hearts,

veiled from the gaze of faithless eyes.

You said:

"Trust our simple hearts,

believe in our love's flight above desires turned to stone."

I have transcended self,

and soared even higher,

ever higher,

until I reached your embrace.

I have tasted the thrill of being, of love.

How dreary my existence was without you,

in the depths of damp earth,

amidst clammy roots, I grew cold.

Oh, how generous you are,

stay with me!

Spring burgeons within our love,

and the birds return from their migration

to each sealed window's sill,

their songs heralding

to caged companions the promise of release.

from "Songs of the Soil"

April 10, 1987 - Karachi

Struggle

Though she couldn't believe
in the secret chamber of her desires,
behind an open window,
two women sit,
both agitated, aflame,
entwined in the tug-of-war between death and life.
Two flames in one hearth,
each vying for the warmth of the other.

One of them, a soulless specter,
has lain for years on the deathbed
of a man who once cloaked her
in the guise of familiar love,
long, long ago.

And the other,
in a bed burdened by societal shame and sin,
where fleeting love rained down
for men passing like whispers,
riding the wild beats of hooves,
giving her stunning nakedness,
a tempestuous gift in the storm of desire.

Yes, inside her, deep within,
behind a narrow window framed with snow,

two worried women watch intently:
one, a hapless plaything of times gone by,
paying the price of a love
long dead within her;
silently, she sits on an old bench of love gone cold,
waiting at the door,
a hookah in her hand, a sip of bitter coffee,
fading softly as an echo of memory.

And the other woman,
who lavishes love on her
and on her cravings—
that woman who yearns for youth,
like a naked tigress in unbridled love,
for each man and woman,
pawing tenderly at the glass of her window.

Yes, within her,
behind these lips sealed in silence,
two women engage in relentless battle:
one sits in peace, clothed in the garments of piety,
aging in the heart of her home,
while the other rises, restless and bare in her heart-home,
regretting every moment
passing without love, without memory,
rubbing her longing forehead against every windowpane,

haunted by the echoes of what might have been.

"In Exile," September 15, 2016

Surge of Silence

A moment of quiet, a surge of unrest,

an assault on you and the beliefs you hold dear,

leaving nothing to chance,

a brutal slaying of silence, every rebellion.

A resurrection for the dead,

from the soil's embrace, from the heart's abyss,

rebels risen, linking the living,

each a chain-link in turn.

A tempest brews,

the wind's magical dance in the sails.

A fleeting instant, no more,

before belief settles at dusk.

Why don't the others see that no chain will lose a link

when the dead rise up

and the uprising begins?

A stillness prevails,

the pretext for a surge.

From the collection "Songs of Ecstasy"
Toronto - June 1990

Tears of Seashell

What can one say:
"I have descended from a sky so pure,
nowhere is bluer,
and each tiny star seems
like an unshed tear?"

What can one express:
"I have lived at the end of a seashell,
which craved each drop of my grief,
to be churned into pearls,
adding to the ocean's wealth.
What words can be conjured?"

What can one reveal:
"I have perched upon waves that roam
over distant foothills,
blooming each drop of my blood
into fresh poppies?"

Yes, I have grown from blood-soaked soil
on the alluring land of a country
that wishes each of its fallen
to be the morning dew,
turning its unwept skin
into a dawn-kissed cloud across the heavens.

***

And now here,

on the land where the sky does not share the hue of the sea,

shells resemble abandoned lairs,

waves grow weary from their tireless journey,

embracing a calm demise.

Here,

under a sky with no balm of cloud,

amid innumerable stars

that resemble shards of glass,

by the grave of no fallen warrior,

the petal of a poppy grows,

and I, ensnared

in the cocoon of my solitude,

a tear unshed in the eye,

a bowl of blood in the heart,

bearing the weight of a saddle on my back,

await the ridge of a horse

that I lost to the tidal wave

in a night so dark,

in a night so silent.

From the collection "In Exile"

October 1, 2006

The Unsaid

How furiously fall
clouds of alienation and sorrow,
and a merciless fog yawns heavy,
with the weight that burdens my breast.
Alas!
Waves upon waves of deep, profound memories
drag the ground from under me into the ocean's abyss,
taking me along.

There's a word in my heart that yet remains
unspoken through the fog and heft of this soul-searing exile.
In my heart, a word whispers—
"Continuous downpours may cast
unripe fruits upon the soil, but
none shall ever taste of their former raw bitterness."

In this estrangement and grief,
within my heart, lies that word.

From the collection "Songs of the Earth"
1987 - Karachi

Testimony

In solitude, I stand alone,

shattering the silence of every platform—

the cold hush in every corner, you see—

bearing witness to my own isolations,

and to a generation that walked beside me.

I testify to the essence of humanity,

where none are truly

the true offspring of another.

I bear witness to the alienation that clings to this dust,

to hearts, companionless,

fading like whispers into memory.

Thus, I cried out from the depths,

fearful of this estrangement,

petrified by the loneliness that dwells within.

Frightened,

not of a love that approaches—

infiltrating every wound I nurture,

an indisputable love, so overflowing,

so hollow and life-devouring,

that it seeks to empty me of myself with every breath.

It is not the love that inflicts another wound upon the flesh,

nor the love that,

though perhaps no less futile,

still grants life its fleeting meaning, that I fear.

My true fear lies in exile,
in the alienation that grips my soul.

from the collection "Lost in the Wind"
April 1998, Toronto

The Cross

Like the Messiah himself,
a vision of love crucified.

A crown of thorns presses upon the heart,
a longing wound for a gentle touch,
etched upon the palm.
A heavy cross to bear,
mourners on either side,
hidden from the world's smiling eyes.

Break the chains from your feet
in your unconstrained love,
for each evening seals the promise of a last kiss.

Behold!
The nobility of Mary's gaze,
in a body aching for her child,
and her passionate weeping.

Open wide your embrace,
the wind carries deceitful thoughts.
And the seductive beauties linger not
out of vain hope
upon the cross of a faithful love
in the evening's shadowed courtyard.

Shame climbs with the moon
through narrow windows,
and love, ever preceding, smiles.

From the collection "Songs of Ecstasy"
August 1987 - Karachi

Times There Are

Times there are when everything, everyone
demands you sever ties and depart.
Pack the chest, traverse, move beyond—
for in the depths of their unmotivated hearts,
you've grown into solitude.

There are moments when all you've desired,
the seeds you've entrusted to the earth,
once hopeful for a life-giving sprout,
crafted through tireless effort
in others' watchful eyes,
now crumble into ruin.

There are times when breaking away is essential,
sowing anew what you've harbored within,
giving birth to your personal deity.
When paths are shrouded,
and leaving, cutting ties, becomes fate's decree.

Times when you stand utterly alone,
estranged within your own being,
a persistent fear that fertilizes
the transparency of its form
within your walled-in soul.

One must go,

for the small stars are waiting,

stars before which the sun dims,

like a flickering, fading light.

One must go,

for today, the sky weeps tears of rain.

The sky pours out grief alongside me.

One must go.

Rain sets the scene for goodbyes.

My heart is heavy with these imposing clouds;

it's as if no one has ever truly known me,

as if no one ever recognized me in their lifetime.

My face, I've surrendered to the void of memory—

no mirrors reside here,

save for the gleaming windows

occupied by strangers gazing out.

One must go,

for today, the sky rains down its sorrows.

Today, the sky grieves with me.

From the collection "In Search of My Land"

May 30, 2018

Tulips in Shackles

Spring heralds its arrival,

Spring's canvas unfolds.

Yet, oh my heart!

No bud nor verdure invades the fortress cold.

Spring rushes in,

eager to restore,

but for the bound affianced, no soothing rose alights their stare—

merely scars left by the crimson lash laid bare.

Exult, companions,

step lively in your mirth.

For every stripe upon the bosom of the lovelorn

carves streams of tulips, red and earth.

And if from the gallows, upon their worn visages,

glow a mille of moon-kissed blossoms, it is not forlorn.

For the hearts of the cherished, in the vernal air,

spring emerges, promising to repair.

Two Haikus

One

Youth passes by,

Two birds perch upon the roof—

Desire sparks a flame.

**Two*

The last leaf stands lone,

Autumn's path aglow with gold—

Reject such demise.

Tremor

Once more, the earth convulsed,
and countless hearts of people quivered.
The earth quaked.
The crimson hands of the divine
trembled with the insignia of this absurd slaughter.

From every corner of this soil,
anguish, tears, and grief arose,
and the voices of the people, this time,
resonated closer to the ears, proclaiming:
"We reject your condolences,
we reject elegies and mourners;
we yearn for aid from your hands."

Our departed have fled,
escaping the torment of this malevolent land.
We, bound and captive to this soil,
seek solace from your hands.

Our living, alas, entombed,
our children, alas, homeless, famished, and adrift;
our mothers weep.

We, the survivors,
yearn not for elegies, tears, and laments.

We yearn for dignity, abodes, and sustenance.

By Bijan Pedram

From the anthology "Quest for My Homeland
November 12, 2017
In mourning of the recent earthquake in Iran.

The Golden Path

The wind whispers from all sides, longing to roam,
and sorrow, too, shall fade away and die.
But love, the bond between us, firmly will stand,
and like a field of wheat, it shall rise—
a blaze against the night's dark sky.

A gentle breeze breathes from every quarter,
combing through the harvest of your hair,
while the sweet scent of your smile
is carried on its shoulders, wide and bare.

Whichever way this current may stray,
it scatters a road of gilded grains
upon a bed of memories, over tombs,
seeding the past with golden remains.

From the collection "Songs of the Earth"
January 1988 - Karachi

Tears of Quietude

All spoke but a weeping girl,
whom they had seen on a dark night,
carried away by a breeze
to a distant land,
to a small patch of soil,
beside another tomb.

Oh, beautiful girl of a faraway place,
sitting by a weeping window,
what can I possibly say to you?
That your tears fall upon his heart and soul,
igniting them with fire,
as the breeze takes him away
to the land of lost nests on earth.

From the collection "Melodies of Longing",
July 1988, Toronto

Turmoil

What disarray lurks deep within my soul,

resisting all attempts at tranquility,

weeping like storm clouds in my chest?

What chaos, O Divine,

with the talon of a fearsome creature,

relentlessly inflicts wounds upon the shattered harp of my heart?

What sorrow haunts me, compelling me

to seek lost loves against my will,

with every breath? What kind of love is this, O God?

From the collection "Melodies of Longing"

Autumn 1988

The Clutch of Dread

My dread, it was,

that the shadowed path of night pursued my timid strides

toward a friend's warm abode.

And within this fear that nestled in my heart,

I circled a radiant orb

of memories from so long ago—

laughter and whispers wrapped in twilight's glow,

Oh, my dear companion!

Till the wind whisked me away...

From the anthology Seeking My Homeland

February 21, 2021

The House of the Beloved

An azure, cloudless sky,
a sky where no heart's urge to fly—
no path to lead me by
to the door of my friend's high abode.

Amidst sap-green trees on the stretch of art,
branches reaching from this realm, astray—
deprived branches yearning for a nest,
longing for that inaugural flight
over roofs, above my beloved friend's home.

Yet on this painted stage,
figures of clay people move,
each shattered vessel mourning a secret sorrow—
salt-flesh beings and coral stone,
entrapped fossils passing by,
devoid of any wish to meet—
not a sound, not a glance,
nor the sweet call of a heart
falls from this domain to the ear.

Ask not of this framework,
where lies the friend's house?
No one knows,
nor does anyone desire

to seek news of the friend.

No rider on the road,
no steed to mount,
to traverse town by town
in search of what is lost.

Across this sprawling canvas,
an artwork of oil and hues,
where no neighbor senses
the heartbeat of another.

Upon this wide expanse,
where the songs of sparrows and doves are gone,
the sky remains unblemished blue—
no cloud to rain today,
no horse or rider to tread every path
to gather tales of my friend's home.

And no soul possesses the urge
to seize a basket of colors and a brush
to sketch a vision of the friend's quarters,
or the steadfast steed
that would bear you to the warm, affectionate heart
of the friend I seek.

The sky, a serene blue,

upon this canvas I speak of,

colored by oil and pigment—

no heart yearns for the sight of another;

the friend's abode is no longer to be found.

From the collection "In Exile,"

March 30, 2016.

The Little Prince

From distant realms, frigid winds sweep,
memories forgotten, chilled breezes seep,
the weight of locked desires, their burden steep.

Silence, a dagger's wound upon my lips,
inflicted by my own hand's brutal eclipse,
etched upon my back, the pain persists.

Winter's allure, a chilling embrace,
no home spared from its icy grace,
within my heart, sharp icicles encase.

Frozen, detached from solitude's bed,
each dawn brings fresh wounds, countless and spread,
from meteor showers, bloody and red.

A distant galaxy cast me into the night,
to this forsaken planet, tears and deceitful smiles ignite,
in that vibrant land, memories fade from sight.

I still see my mother's vibrant face,
in that distant galaxy's embrace,
my father's grave, a cold stone's trace.

Brothers' playful mischief, memories alive,

sisters' love affairs with neighborhood boys they strive,
people on rooftops, hearts unconfined.

In that vibrant land, names forgotten,
like my mother's own, abandoned one cold night,
left behind, alone—a solitary plight.

Upon a dark comet, they wandered afar,
leaving me behind, a solitary star,
in dreams, I sce three bright green stars.

Above this doomed planet, I perish in plight,
emerging from a distant galaxy's light,
in dreams, three shining emeralds ignite.

My mother's smiles in the lullaby of her eyes,
fragrant orange blossoms, intoxicating melodies arise,
behind laughter's lips, a dream that never dies.

In dreams, deep rivers of time flow through space,
golden waves, thousands of stars embrace,
ancient moments, I soar like a fish in flight's grace.

Crystal-clear waters, milky rivers wide,
three small red fish join my dance's stride,
twisting serpents release, venom's sweetness beside.

From this vulnerable body, a burden let go,
entwined with swirling comets' frenzied glow,
before dawn's arrival, awakening's call, we know.

A venomous bite, setting me free,
like honey's cup, from chains I flee,
shackles of this mortal frame no longer decree.

Upon the bed, suffering's slow death bore,
with dreams and metaphors, I shall explore—
the Little Prince, forevermore.

Oh, land forgotten, lost in time,
galaxy of dreams where memories chime,
oh, joyful mother, your homeland sublime.

Adorned with agates, your land did gleam,
sky lit by ten suns, a radiant theme,
green stars and pearls, a nightly regime.

On rocks to the sea, men rode with grace,
swift horses carried them to embrace,
loved ones awaited at doorsteps' embrace.

Men, like hard rocks, found solace in sleep,
beautiful women, smiles fresh and deep,
leopard lineage, women's souls to keep.

Birds in meadows and plains took flight,
surpassing men's stature, reaching great height,
children gifted windows, shining bright.

Shooting stars shattered glass with might,
the wind carried their flight, hearts alight,
combing hair in clouds, children's delight.

And here I am, a shattered frame,
no longer me, trapped in this nameless claim,
on a frozen planet, venomous sting to tame.

Snakes' venom, the only path to free,
from the slow grip of death, destiny's decree—
in this prisoned body, I long to flee.

"In Exile's embrace"
September 15, 2016

The Kiss

A kiss, a sip of pure delight,
a pomegranate's yearning on eager lips—
the sun's warm blood,
veiled in chambers of the heart's abyss.

A kiss, like grapes, tastes of sweet,
passion's beads, warm and sugary, in death's wine—
it is love's blood, moon's essence, stone's design,
wordless melodies flowing through time's embrace.

A kiss is a birth,
a union of waterfall and its roar—
captivating, an eternal mirth.

Your kiss, a symphony upon my lips,
a gentle fire of shyness, my skin's bloom,
a sun unruly, lush with passion's spree,
defiant against the gloom of loneliness.

The Labyrinth of Fate

Every soul, every being, treads a path,
With roads that climb and fall in rhythmic wrath.
From deep springs to stirring riverside,
Where pebbles and slopes decide
The course of their tumultuous ride.

Each entity holds a destined fate,
A path chosen, laden with weight and guile.
A daunting journey forged on their own,
More than the fates that have been overthrown,
Destinies thoughtless, from the end they've grown.

But my spring, my beloved one,
Springs forth from my heart's own sun.
A beauty unsurpassed, born of you,
Seeking a way through the labyrinth of your form,
To uncover desires that are your class,
To quench my heart's yearning for your daily glass.

A river with rises and rapturous falls,
Chosen by me before any other calls.
My destiny intertwined in your embrace,
A passionate chase, a dance of souls,
Together we navigate the twists and turns,
As our love forges a path that forever burns.

From the collection "In Exile"

October 2, 2016

The Love Orchard

Without you, tears;
with you, smiles.
Without you, a burned land;
with you, a flourishing forest.

On your bare shoulder rests a white bird,
fearless of traps and snares,
feeding on the seeds of passion.

Silence takes form in your absence,
while the hum of love lingers in your hands' caress.
Neither the expanse of the deep sky is vaster than your heart,
nor is my flight broader than your shoulders.

Where are you, my friend,
to bloom upon heart and door
with a secret blush upon your cheeks?
Arise, for the night without you is boundless;
arise, for the day flourishes in your presence.

The sun at the end of every night
waits for your eyes to rise.
My friend,
all begins with you,
and love is the song of your heart.

In the silent infinity of night,

without you, tears;

with you, smiles.

Without you, a barren land;

with you, a vibrant forest.

To Shida with Love

 For our first anniversary April 30, 1988 - Toronto

Transient Turmoil

In perpetual flux, nothing finds its rest.

Not the weeping clouds shrouded in their somber veil,

nor the radiant sun that scatters light, setting worlds ablaze.

Not the shifting sands draping your dormant figure,

nor the lifeless fish adrift upon the tide,

nor the myriad jagged peaks,

nor my own blurred, languid reflection.

We evade each other,

crash inward,

all of us succumbing to the fall.

Surrender to the ceaseless stir—

to departure, to fracture, to ashes in the wind,

to be swept wherever whims may lead.

Tarry here and watch,

as coffee grows tepid, untouched.

Time eludes—

grief fades away,

joy follows in its fleeting steps,

as dreams dissolve into the ether.

All you hold dear, in an instant,

flitters past.

Make haste!

Consider, if you will,

that even death is transient,

and you, too, shall fade from memory.

Your heart no longer your own,

nor the soil beneath your feet,

where none can inherit your love.

Upon fruitful limbs, pomegranates wither—

yet reach for them,

pluck the crimson sweetness they harbor.

Birds in infinite passages shift,

grasp your heart, bleeding yet bold, and ascend.

Embrace the relentless unrest;

for in stillness, there lies death,

and even death stirs with restlessness.

From "In Search of My Land"

November 15, 2017

The Sun's Embrace

The sun sought me, a wanderer up until dawn;
the sun came to me.
I asked it, "Oh friend, do you know,
with my eyes' gaze you're no longer the same,
gentle and charming?

Do you comprehend that throughout the night,
my vigilant eyes engaged in battle
with the haunting might of darkness?
My body scorched in fever's blight,
yearning for your arrival at my door,
to cast your warm glow upon my chilled core,
to ignite a glimmer of hope once more
in my tormented heart—do you grasp?

But now, as my heart is ravaged by demise,
in the stark darkness of this unveiled night,
you return,
gently tapping on every frost-sealed windowpane.
You've led me to despair, yet I shall not disappoint you,
for the radiance of your light—
how magnificently you shine.

Indeed, although this heart is ensnared by night's depths,
in that crucible moment of farewell,

when you will no longer appear,

still, I won't bestow despair upon you.

Others still anticipate your arrival, my old friend;

for the radiance of your light—

how splendidly you illuminate.

The Serenade of Cicadas

Cicadas serenade,

guiding me on a tune

to the heart of a humble homestead,

where stood my father,

siblings,

mother, grandmother—

whom their memories sweetened my existence.

Their chants echo

through the softening hush of night,

a melody of love and laughter

that weaves through the fabric of time.

I move beyond moments,

spanning immeasurable gaps,

to converge with vivid recollections

entwined with the cricket's hymn,

the swallow's melody,

and the gentle psalms of rain

mingling with the ardent hold of earth.

"Exile Notes,"
November 17, 2016

The End

In silence pure, so vast and empty,
Where no memories dare to dwell,
Upon your violet peaks, they rest—
Rings of pleasure, pain, and parting—
Circles of love and separation,
Symbols of trust and betrayal.

Years slip by with gentle hands,
Vanished in a fleeting day,
Entwined in loops upon your breast;
A hand like sun's radiant embrace,
On icy relics, frozen fast,
Where warmth and frost in silence blend.

Cry out from deep within your soul,
Yet no one hears, no savior near,
No shared outcry, no end goal—
No start, no finish to this fear.
Cry out, unleash your roaring breath,
In this wasteland, God is gone,
And Satan too, a nameless death,
In endless life, we wander on,
Confounded in the timeless haze,
Lost in our unending maze.

The rings grow tighter, pain's sweet sting,
To marrow deep, it creeps and clings,

For feasting on the worms below,

It sweetens life with bitter throes—

A shared pain, though lonely, sunk,

In shadows where our spirits flunk.

Fear not the solitude and loss,

Years spent beneath your shadow's sway,

And all that in your being was.

Did you not see, at what cost,

That exile blossoms from within?

Within you flows a silent stream,

Draining to valleys deep and wide,

In search of cries, a distant dream,

Amidst a silence that won't bide.

Man is alone,

God is alone,

Your beloved too, in shadows grown.

The only bond we share, this plight—

The pain of loneliness in flight,

A shadow trailing ever near,

In pursuit of what we fear.

Cry out from deep within your soul,

In this world, so bare, so bleak,

No one's here to hear your toll.

Our journey's start from ending spun;

One day will come when I am gone,

But echoes of my love remain,

In circles woven, joy and pain—
A symbol of love and death's embrace.

July 2024

Until You Arrive

In your absence, my love, upon my dwelling's crest,

there's no dance of smoke to warm the air,

nor in my small garden, a leafy zest.

Brick upon brick I lay, stone upon stone,

awaiting the moment you tread through the door,

to share a meal upon my hearthstone,

scattering seeds of your smile on the earthen floor.

With your arrival,

I will comb my hair's velvet sheen,

and rest my heart upon a plate of cloud,

laid bare, yearning for your gaze, my dear.

Brick by brick, I build a sanctuary,

stone upon stone,

until the day you enter from without.

From the collection "Songs of Fervor"

April 1988 - Toronto

Until Another Winter

And at last...

From the bosom of a fallen leaf,

a sigh arose,

vanishing within the hueless mist,

in the lingering illusions of a distant cloud.

No trace of it remained,

nor did it harbor in its heart

any will to leave a mark,

save for a damp reverie

of the life-giving dread of the sun,

in the withering thought of a leaf.

The fall of a single leaf

is not the forest's denudation,

nor is the rising dew,

nor the conception of a cloud,

a sign of the sea's desiccation.

For in kindness,

upon the soil's mournful affliction,

the growling clouds bestow their rain,

and colored dewdrops

on the buds of verdant shrubs

await the sun's embrace.

Do not despair!
Should the capricious hand of the wind
stir up thousands of moaning leaves
upon the earth.

Do not fear!
If within the cloud's infertile conceit,
thousands of weeping dewdrops
await the cold red dawn
with the memory of loved ones.
And if the cloud holds back its rain,

do not lose hope!
If birds perish,
and others in their memory lament,
for with every spring,
thousands of love-struck birds
will embark upon this silent forest's embrace.

Under the Enigmatic Night

Beneath the night's abyssal cloak,

I've traced the path where your feet evoke

the moon's ethereal roots that shimmer bright,

unquestionably radiant, divinely aligned.

With grace, you stand, a celestial bloom,

as beams of light dance around you,

silently eluding the crimson haze.

I choose to tread a trail of tears and rays,

where shadows play and whispers twine,

a gentle embrace, so sublime.

And on your lips, a sun-kissed smile

paints the darkness with warmth and style,

amidst this night's enigmatic embrace,

where longing lingers in every heart.

Vanished Dignity

I chase whispers of you, uncaught,
a specter in the roar of thunder,
glinting off mountaintops, causing a sudden shiver,
like a seedling's murmur in the hush of hidden waters.

I reach for traces of you, scattered,
a breaker of stillness in the depths,
a painter with a palette of rivers golden,
wandering through the silent pines, long slumbering.

I thirst for fleeting sips,
kissed by sun's fire, sea's embrace,
voicing marble-bold, yet a libertine's grace,
bathing in sunbeams, diving into the tide,
singing with a choir that sways, boundless and wide.

I hunger for your motion, forward thrust,
spinning the valiant to the fray's cusp,
yet cradling love tightly in war's fierce clutch.

Amidst the rain's cadence, I search for you,
the spell of verdant splendor beckoning,
pure shimmer that tips the morning dew,
a dignity once whole, now for understanding, beckoning.

Veils

Between twin hearts' narrowed gap,
dark veils hanging heavy and somber.
In gaze's depth, on branch's arc,
a perched bird's pause,
amidst the song of wings to heedful ears,
a ring of light leaps to questing eyes;
on these panes of glass,
dark veils suspend.

My flesh's moist shade,
from night's cold spite unchained,
yearns for your touch's grace,
your gaze,
the warmth of your smile,
in fraught vigil for waking's sharp toll.
Each veil's hidden dread
seizes away your touch's sweet construct
to an expanse untold.

Light cleaves night's bond;
your sunlit essence
strikes at my windowed soul.
I rise,
to fling each window wide,
to sift away the veils;

yet the key—
long since shattered
in these stubborn locks,
leaves me captive
within these clutching walls, these windows,
sequestered till twilight's chill.

A lamp's expired glow
casts formless doubts
on every pane's face.
Before this effigy, broken, I stand,
its essence marred by veil's density,
cloaked within countless folds,
with two dark veils o'er my own sight laid.

Breathless and sundered, I face this guise
that mirrors me
and murmurs my name.

"In Exile"
March 25, 2016

Veil of Desire

Atop the mountain's peak,

Body glistening with the harsh of path,

Winds of desire play, beguiling yet serene.

Though at times, they drag you to an abyss so bleak,

From which escape finds no way,

Yet they're beautiful, deceptive, ever so keen—

Yet relentless breezes

At the mountain's peak

From the collection "Songs of Passion"

January 22, 1988 - Karachi

Veil of Elusiveness

A path elusive, veiled in haze,
Yet vivid as a sunlit maze within my soul.

No forward path, my beloved,
No sight of the road ahead,
For in the warmth of your secure embrace,
A cunning hunter lies in wait,
With bow and arrow, hidden from light.

As bright as a sunbeam in my heart,
The path appeared elusive,
Beneath the refuge of that poignant smile,
Silently blooming,
Caressed by the deceptive stroke of the brush
Upon the marble wall, unyielding and cold—
That wall of unrelenting stone,
Setting me apart from the rest.

Under the sanctuary of your captivating smile,
So tender, so gentle,
Yes, that smile that graces your lips,
Exuding utmost compassion,
Yet firepits and pitfalls linger unseen.

It seemed there was no pathway,

My companion,

With a heart as clear as daylight.

Vermilion Bloom

Oh, if I might

pluck my cheek from its perch and lay it upon the fervent caresses

shed from the sanctuary of your affection,

dispersed, dancing lightly o'er my countenance.

I could, if I could only believe,

trust in the vivid blooms

birthed in the aftermath of your embrace,

defying the pulsing skepticism cradled in my heart.

I could, if only I dared to dream.

Void

Oh, love, a force that lifts me beyond the sky,

and pain, an enigmatic visitor to my soul's depths.

Without you, I'm a drifting vessel in the unknown;

with you, I become the song, a whispered melody.

Legends speak of unseen powers,

whispers claim solace amidst chaos.

Yet I tread cautiously, never fully believing,

for trust in transient human beliefs is but fleeting.

Not of known elements or realms,

I am the offspring of winds that dance unseen,

soaring over the embers of unspoken fires.

My heart twirls amid the sparks' embrace,

seeking echoes of that fervent longing.

The vernal breeze murmurs its elusive secrets;

the cloud weeps in an endless cascade of emotions.

My heart chills, distanced from its core,

if it falters on the winding path to your envisioned dreams.

Voyage

The journey from the homeland,
a mournful kiss
tarnishing life's lips.
The harrowing tune of a stone's lament,
sinking into the unguarded heart of a sparrow,
settling in blood.

The fragility of a goblet
that fell to earth and shattered.
Drenched humans,
forlorn, soaked by the rain of misfortune,
contemplate the abject moments of their existence,
and whatever limits them—
focused not on what should have been theirs,
nor what they should have done.

A bowl overflowing with shame resides in me.
I feel myself drifting away
from something that, day by day, makes me more fragile,
like thinning porcelain walls of rebellion within me,
until, from the trembling terror in a bird's heart,
I splinter,
spilling to the ground.

Yet the journey

is the saddest kiss of all.

We Are Legion

In the parched veins of earth,
the ants are many,
echoing our own multitude.
Scattered along the silent seashore,
the sands stretch infinitely,
mirroring our existence.
Dangling on the dark chest of night,
the stars abound,
shimmering like our distant dreams.

Yet we are neither ant nor grain,
nor luminous celestial bodies
in the dark night.
We are,
nameless, insignia-less dead,
anonymous as an ant,
solitary as a whisper of sand in the wind,
as obscure as an unlit night.

We lie in this dark soil,
clinging to vain hope
that someone may rise
and awaken us
from our bed of slumber.
We are the living interred,

yearning for the light of freedom.

We,
insignificant creatures
in our own unwindowed human cocoon.

From the collection "In Search of My Land"
February 23, 2021

Wheat field

Oh, how I wish
upon a distant trail of dust,
in the wake of a heart-kindling breeze,
toward the abode of my beloved
I was adrift.

Oh, how I wish
with the hope for a fresh sprout,
hidden amidst the dancing wheat spikes,
beneath the watchful gaze of my dear friend—
I was amazed.

Sometimes I muse
upon my verdant skin, so forlorn;
branches sprout solo, craving—
a thousand tiny pores obscure
yearning for a breeze that kisses
the face of my beloved,
to find a path into my soul.

And every now and then I perceive
the narrow straits my throat bears,
channeling the hum of the wind
and the warmth of the earth
through the withered veins of reed beds.

Oh, friend!

On a sun-drenched, distant path,

in the continuum of your home,

I find meaning in life,

and the road is a riddle

entwining bones and hearts buried in the earth

beneath the beaming sun.

My beloved, how I wish,

with a burden on my back,

shoulder to shoulder with this heart that was but is no longer mine—

in your migration,

I was with you

in the whisper of a breeze that sweeps us,

soaring together to the distant seas.

How I wish...

Whispers of Neglect

The note was brief and cold,

A dagger poised by a friend's hand,

Piercing the unsuspecting man's back.

"If ever you seek my welfare... I am well, thanks be to God...

What news do you carry... What should one say to you?

I do not know...

These days my mind's engulfed in busyness...

Let me keep this short."

Ellipsis...

And ellipsis again...

More piercing dots—

With a frigid snap, they fractured

The thread of our dialogue,

Exposing, through our neglect,

The tragedy of our amity.

Each unspoken word, a silent scream,

Echoes in the hollow space between us,

A weight of memories left to cry,

Haunted by the silence that binds us apart.

From the collection "Lost in the Wind"

April 1987, Toronto

Windows

Windows open, frames that play,
I speak from an expansive view,
a space as vast as the human spirit,
with delicate roots of connection
to cherished memories of a friend.

Neither the horizon is closer than a reaching hand
that reaches unrestrained,
nor the heart.
Always toward the horizon one must journey,
to that expansive azure realm
where lovebirds soar,
gently gliding over a boundless meadow
between two souls.

One must go,
always one must go.

Winter Passage

I walked by your side through winter's hold,
passed that forest, once merry, now untold,
where not a single leaf's green pulse did unfold.
During a winter so harsh, so piercing and bold,

my timid songs turned into howls untamed,
by winds morphed to wolves' bane,
to panicked cries of a village, plagued by dread,
in dawn's assault, as locust swarms overhead.

When autumn came, it brought a hue,
with all its endless colors anew—
the richness of a love well-known and true.
I understood then, the winter grew,

not from misfortune's sudden call,
but from the womb of our rapport.
Thus, I believed, with unwavering sight,
in the sun's prowess to tease out your smile so bright,

with the gentlest kiss of its warming light.
Each leaf the wind carried away, astray
from your branches, winding in grand ballet,
upon the winter sleep of your form will lay.

Tender shoots will rise, a delicate display,

songbirds chorusing on your outstretched limbs,

turtledoves calling as daylight dims.

I know, a heady spring shall come from the mountain pass,

with the wild heartbeat of your hooves, alas,

upon my wounded chest will mass,

O friend!

"Songs of Passion" January 1988

Witness

Alone, I shattered the silence
of every solitary scaffold,
the cold stillness of each frame I see.
I bore witness to my own loneliness,
and to the ancestral loneliness that lived with me.

I bore witness to the human who is alone,
who never owes their existence
to anyone else.
I bore witness to the exiles of this land,
to hearts wandering without compassion,
fading from memory.

I became the one who cried from within,
for I fear the exile
and the loneliness of the heart.
I fear
not that love which arrives
with every wound it finds within me—a love so full,
meaningless, soul-stirring,
seeking to empty me of myself, each moment.

I fear the exile,
not that love which brings forth
another wound upon the body,

not that love

which, though it may be more meaningless than any other,

nevertheless gives life its meaning.

From the collection "Lost in the Wind"
April 1998 - Toronto

Witnesses to the unseen

With a gaze dropped in fear's embrace,
we witnessed what eyes should evade.
With mouths agape, torn by ache's shout,
we crumbled where we shouldn't have stayed.

And at last, we wept our sorrow-soaked hearts
in the stranger's hold, the one deemed wrong.
If only, oh if only—
speak to me, join my song!

We harbored a hope far mightier still—
to rest in each other's arms,
to weep on trembling shoulders,
in the lonely stir of a drizzle-night's charms.

If only we could unite in this endeavor,
to shed the tears of our aching hearts
in the solace of our embrace.

From the collection "Lost in the Wind,"
On a twilight of 1999

Words Unvoiced

Clouds of exile and sorrow
suffocate as they descend,
and a leaden fog over my heart
yawns wearily.

Though waves of memories
sweep the ground beneath my heart,
dragging me out to sea,
I ponder within—still,
yet there are words within my heart, unspoken,
beneath the heaviness of exile, in this weighty haze.

Though the incessant downpour
knocks immature fruits to the ground,
no fruit shall ever
taste of its unripened yesterday.

In this sorrow, in this foreignness,
I sense a dialogue with my heart.

From the collection "Songs of the Earth"
1987 - Karachi

Wings of Ardor

Stand upon the towering vast,

From your verdant heights, behold

The countless birds beneath, their plight stark and bold.

There, the yearning to be as humans are—

To spread one's wings like theirs,

Sprouts gently at your fingertips' tender care.

My verdant love, unfurl your fervent wings;

The earth lies in wait for your vigor's lull.

Take flight, soar high,

Fly, fly.

From the collection "Songs of Ardor"

June 1987

Yearning in the Boundless Fields

I long to cradle familiar countenances,

softly sweeping away their tearful burdens,

seeking solace in my gentle arms.

Yearning to become the unwavering moon,

radiant and serene,

hovering above, bestowing calm,

shrugging off fear's grasp.

Imagine me as a fish, adorned in shimmering hues,

dancing amidst the moon's silver murmurs,

within waters alive with dreams,

gliding through depths, a guardian of untold secrets.

A melodious bird with wings of emerald takes flight,

chasing elusive, forgotten harmonies,

in a realm where shadows linger.

I soar, a whisper of solace through the starry night.

If only my tears, stained with heartache,

could cascade over these lush, sprawling fields—

a cleansing deluge, banishing the specter of fear,

offering a soothing balm for souls entwined in sorrow's embrace.

Yesterday's Sweet Savor

Oh friend, do you truly grasp
the silent storm you've unleashed within me
when you laid bare
the bitter secrets concealed in your heart?

Do you comprehend, perhaps,
how no fruit shall henceforth retain
the sweetness of yesterday,
after you clawed brutally
into the depths of my being?

You must know,
you'll offer your heart at a time
when mine has ceased to beat with me,
and I am no longer who I once was—
a mere colorless shadow
lingering by your side.

This heart, which is my own,
will be plundered into oblivion,
yearning for someone to recall its tide.
Do you truly grasp
what has transpired within me?

From the collection "Lost in the Wind"

July 2003

Your Exquisite Hands

Alas,
I was not present
where your beautiful hands
melted away, drop by drop,
and the constant rain's elixir
carried them along.

Your alluring hands,
swept away by unveiled streams,
were taken from me.
Thus, in all the waters of the world,
and in springs born from the earth's heart,
your hands flowed.

And the birds in love,
on their trepidatious migration,
drank from the palms of your hands
to weave songs of longing.

***

Oh, how I wished to be there,
where my lips' yearning for kisses
upon your tender hands
could have opened birds' mouths
to more heartfelt verses.

My beloved,
permit me to weep
in the seclusion of the gloomiest nights,
in that impasse of time
where my frozen hands
find no path to yours.

Let the weeping commence;
perhaps these tears on dark nights
will find their way to your hands.

From the collection "Lost in the Wind"
1998- Toronto

Your hidden Stems

In the depths of night's dark hue,

beneath your radiant feet,

I've sensed the roots of the moon—

tentative stems enhancing light,

coiled in the dark,

wrapped around your body.

Evading the night's blood tricks,

in a labyrinth echoing with tears,

I've sat,

twisting my delicate stems

toward the whirl of your legs,

blooming upon your lips

a sunlit smile,

amidst this midnight's tyranny.

From the collection "Songs of Dust",

Autumn 1987 - Karachi

Your Name

If your name still lingers,
untangled from stone, water, and grass,
unwoven from the steps of a wild gazelle,
or the ethereal glow of the moon's crystal.

If your name remains elusive,
not yet a slippery fish,
gliding through the depths of memory's well,
at the crossroads of apple and meadow.

Fear not, my beloved verdant,
for soon, atop jagged mountain stones,
bathed in the moon's silvery luminescence,
eyes will catch sight of your name etched upon rugged paths,
and the sweet tenderness of your kisses
beneath vibrant green canopies.

They will remember
the verses you forged in twilight,
with hands scarred by treacherous rocks,
so that you may herald the sun's ascent
upon the towering blade of the mountain.

With each step,
your name will dance upon their tongues,

melodious and eternal,

a hymn of love and longing,

echoing through the ages.

Your Stems

In the depths of night's obsidian hue,

beneath your radiant feet,

I've sensed the moon's roots—

gentle stems, illuminating light,

coiling around your body

in the stillness of the dark.

Silently evading the night's blood tricks,

in a labyrinth echoing with suppressed tears,

I've sat,

twisting my delicate stems

toward the whirl of your legs,

blooming upon your lips

a sunlit smile,

amidst midnight's tyranny. –

From the collection "Songs of Dust",

Autumn 1987 - Karachi

Your voice

Your voice, your voice,

that should not be declared,

strangely is not apart from me,

for it dwells even more alien,

yes, the most estranged with me.

Emanating from the channel of your throat,

which never felt the warmth of its gentle breaths

against the chill of my skin,

your voice—

that should not be spoken of—

is not just acquainted with me,

but much closer—

indeed, the closest to me.

In the most secluded nights,

when enchanting caresses of sleep

sought not my weary lids,

and the silence of distant abysses stole me away,

there I have heard

the beautiful melody of your voice

at the dawn of days,

declaring the enduring night a harbinger for wayfarers.

Your voice,

the peculiarly familiar voice.

From the collection 'Lost in the Wind'
1999 - Toronto